Contents

Section 1 — Water 1

Section 2 — Local Traffic 7

Section 3 — A Seaside Town 13

Section 4 — The Mountain Environment 19

Section 5 — Investigating Coasts 25

Section 6 — Passport to the World 33

Section 7 — Geography, Maps and Numbers 37

The Answers 42

Published by CGP
Written by
Gary Betcherman
Mark Ollis

Typesetting, Design and Graphics by
Martin Chester, Sandy Gardner, Sharon Keeley,
Becky May and Rachel Selway
With thanks to Glenn Rogers *and* Mark Haywood *for the Proofreading.*

Maps reproduced from Ordnance Survey mapping by permission of the Ordnance Survey on behalf of the Controller of Her Majesty's Stationary Office, © Crown copyright, License No. 100034841.

ISBN: 978 1 84146 751 1

Groovy Website: www.cgpbooks.co.uk
Printed by Elanders Ltd, Newcastle upon Tyne.
Jolly bits of clipart from CorelDRAW®.

Based on the classic CGP style created by Richard Parsons.

Psst... photocopying this Workbook isn't allowed, even if you've got a CLA licence. Luckily, it's dead cheap, easy and quick to order more copies from CGP – just call us on 0870 750 1242. Phew!

Text, design, layout and original illustrations © Coordination Group Publications Ltd. (CGP) 2003
All rights reserved.

Section 1 — Water

Where Is Water Found?

Some places in the world have plenty of water, while others have hardly any at all.

1 Complete the map's key by filling in the boxes with the correct colours.

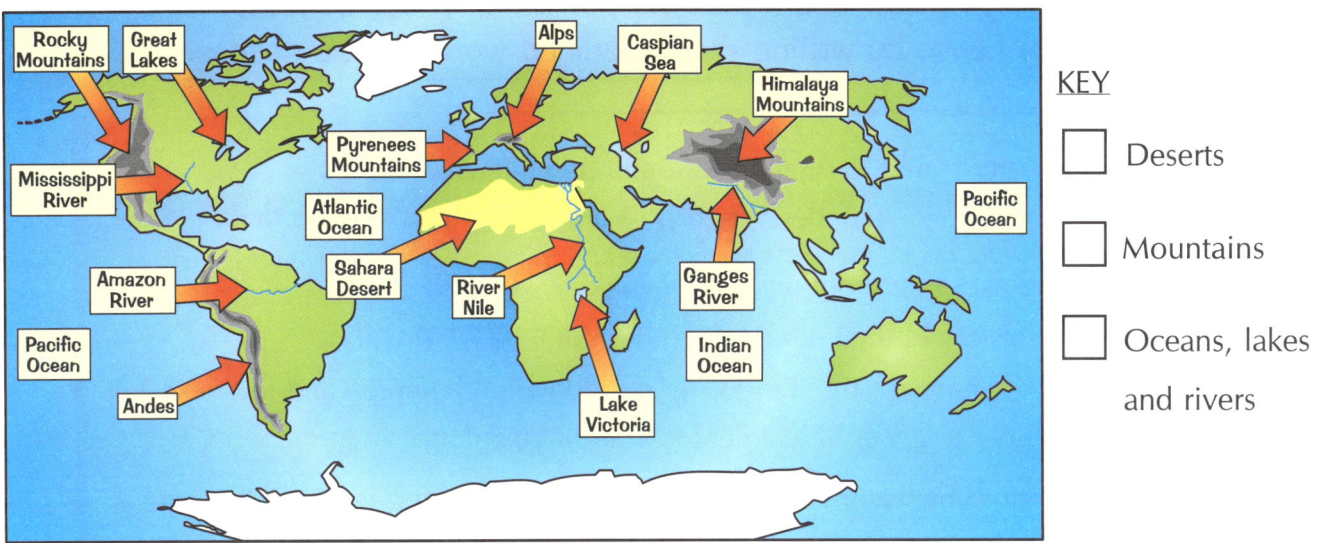

KEY

☐ Deserts

☐ Mountains

☐ Oceans, lakes and rivers

2 Cross out the wrong words in the paragraph below.

Most of the water in the world is in the **LAKES / OCEANS**, but we can't drink that water because it's too **SALTY / FISHY**. The water on the tops of many mountains can't be used because it's **FROZEN / HIDING**. Not many people live in deserts because there isn't enough **SUNSHINE / RAIN** to grow food.

3 Which sources of water move and which just stand?
Write each source of water in the correct part of the table.

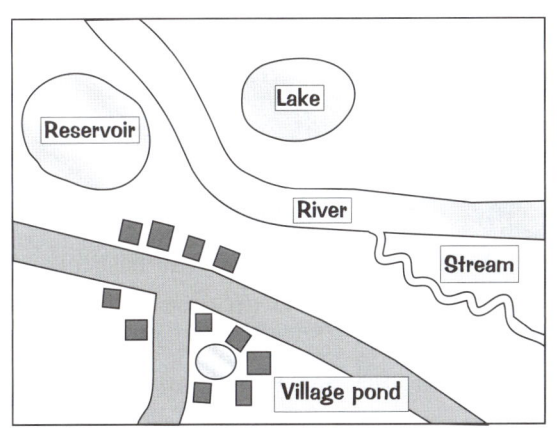

Use the map to help you.

Sources

River   Reservoir   Pond
Lake   Stream

Moving Water	Standing Water

Most people live fairly near to lakes or rivers — not many people live in places without much water.

Section 1 — Water

How Do We Get Our Water?

Most people don't live right next to water, so their water must be brought to them — and taken away again after it's been used.

1 Read the passage below about how we get water in our houses. Then label the house by writing the underlined words in the spaces.

☆1☆ Clean water comes to my house from a **pumping station**. It comes through an underground pipe and is kept in a **storage** tank.

☆2☆ Pipes take water from the storage tank to where it's needed. You have to turn on a **tap** to get the water out of the pipe.

☆3☆ After it's been used, the dirty water goes down a drainpipe and into a **sewer**. Next it goes to a waste treatment centre for cleaning.

☆4☆ When it rains, the water from the roof collects in a **gutter** and goes through a **drainpipe** and into the ground. This water helps to keep the grass in the garden healthy. If it doesn't rain enough I water the grass with a **hosepipe**.

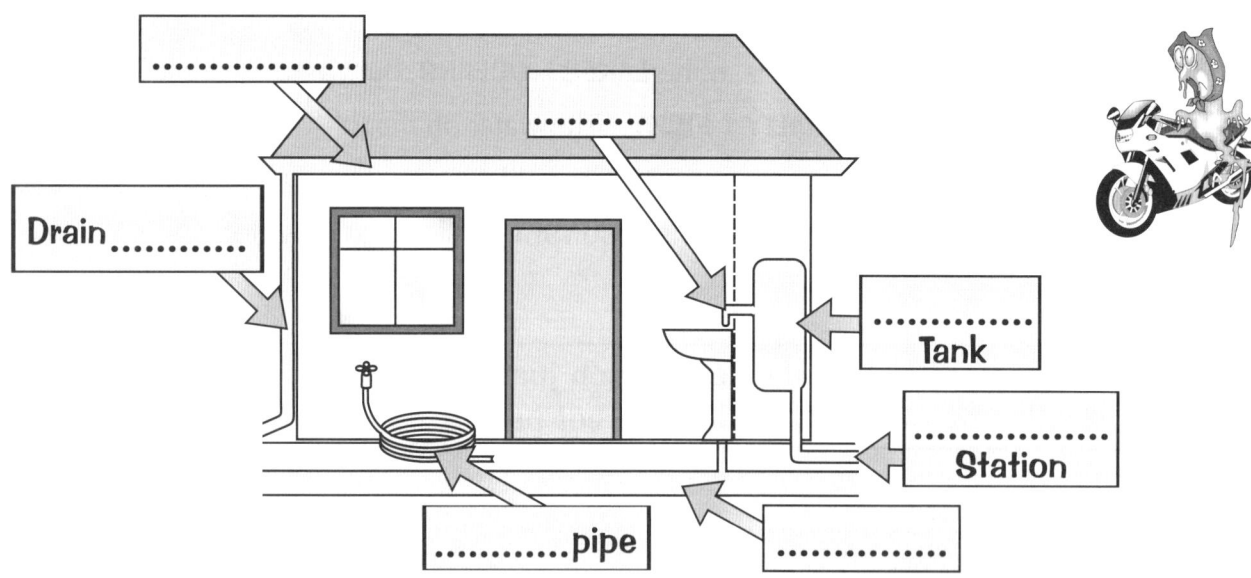

2 Put a tick in the box beside the best way of irrigating crops.

Irrigation = when it doesn't rain enough, farmers bring water to the fields to help their crops grow.

☐ Use a water pistol.
☐ Pump water in through pipes.
☐ Walk around and cry over the plants.
☐ Borrow an elephant to squirt water at the crops.

Most of the water we use travels through pipelines to where it's needed...

Section 1 — Water

Uses of Water

Everybody needs water to stay alive. We are lucky and can get our water from a tap, but in some parts of the world people have to travel long distances to get their water.

1 Tick the two things these women in Africa will use their water for.

☐ cooking
☐ drinking
☐ washing the car

It takes them more than two hours every day to fetch water from the nearest well.

2 Water is used for many things besides drinking. Draw lines to match up the uses of water with their correct headings.

| Home | Leisure | Farming | Industry |

watering crops   cooking rice   steam engine   swimming

3 Use the words coming out of the tap to fill in the gaps in the sentences below.

Mum did a load of .... while Dad washed up the dirty ....

Mum .... the kitchen floor while Dad .... the car.

Dad .... the plants while Mum .... spaghetti.

While Dad took a ...., Mum had a cup of tea.

watered, shower, cooked, washed, dishes, mopped, laundry

<u>ACTIVITY:</u> Write a list of all the different ways you used water yesterday.

Section 1 — Water

Wasting Water

...ds of things, so it's important not to waste it.

... the box to complete the sentences about saving water at home.

> plants   clothes   kettle
> pipes   shower

Mum only puts as much water as she needs in the .... when making a cup of tea.

Dad uses the leftover water from cooking to water the .... in the house.

Mum waits until there are enough dirty .... to fill the machine before doing a load of laundry. Dad takes a .... instead of a bath.

They both check once a week that no .... are leaking.

2 Tick the sentences that describe water being wasted in a school.

a) ☐ Taps not being closed all the way after hands are washed.
b) ☐ Getting a glass of water when you're thirsty.
c) ☐ Leftover water from lunch being used to water plants.
d) ☐ Children filling balloons with water to throw at other children.

3 Circle the correct words to complete these sentences.

Pumping water out of rivers uses up a lot of **custard / energy / eggcups**. Large reservoirs to store water use up a lot of **bath tubs / sheep / land**.

> Rivers, lakes and underground wells are natural stores of water. Lots of water is also stored in man-made reservoirs.

ACTIVITY: Write sentences about the different ways you could save water.

Section 1 — Water

Keeping Water Clean

Drinking dirty water can make you very ill — it needs to be cleaned before you can use it.

1 Match up the types of water below to how good they would be to drink.

Green coloured with green slime floating on top. Smells very bad.

Clear. Doesn't smell of anything.

Muddy and unclear. Doesn't smell.

☺ Good to drink

😐 Not very good to drink

☠ Very bad to drink

Some water is too dirty to use — it may have germs in it that make you ill.

2 Circle the things that will be filtered out from water if the holes are this big: ○.

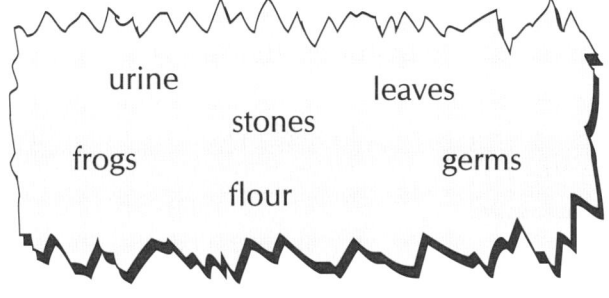

Filtering is when water is poured through tiny holes. Big things can't get through and get left behind.

Not everything can be filtered out — some things are too small.

3 Circle the method below that is most likely to kill any germs in water.

Filter the water   Boil the water to kill the germs   Drink it through a straw

4 Put a number in each box below so that the stages of cleaning water are in the right order.

HINT: In the UK, water is treated before it comes to our taps so we don't have to boil it.

☐ Filter out bad things from the used water.

☐ Return the filtered water to a river.

[1] Take the water from a river.

☐ Pipe the water to people's taps.

☐ Take the used water away from houses.

☐ Treat the water to remove harmful germs.

Sometimes germs in water are so bad that they could kill you if you drank the water...

Section 1 — Water

Who Owns Water?

The water we use falls from the sky as rain, then soaks into the ground, or flows into rivers and lakes. But even though rain is free, you have to pay for water from your taps.

1 Tick the three reasons why water companies charge us for our water, even though they don't own it.

- [ ] Because they know how to make it rain.
- [ ] Because they deliver the water to our taps.
- [ ] Because they make the water in secret labs.
- [ ] Because they clean the water for us.
- [ ] Because they own the clouds.
- [ ] Because they take our used water away.

2 Use words from the box to fill in the gaps in the sentences below.

| wells | ground | crops | clean | flush |

In many poor countries there isn't enough water for people. Poorer countries are often helped by aid agencies and charities.

Many aid agencies and charities help build ....

so that people can get water out of the ....

This means that people can have .... water for drinking and cooking.

They can keep themselves clean and .... away human waste as well.

It also means they have enough to water their ....

and keep their animals healthy.

3 Circle the good things that happen when people have better and cleaner water.

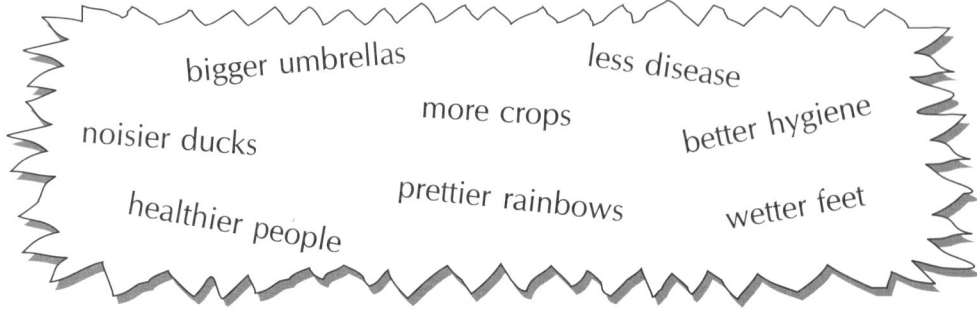

bigger umbrellas   less disease   more crops   noisier ducks   better hygiene   prettier rainbows   wetter feet   healthier people

ACTIVITY: Design a poster asking people to donate money to help supply poorer countries with clean water.

Section 1 — Water

Section 2 — Local Traffic

What is a Town Centre Like?

Town centres are usually busy and full of traffic. There are usually lots of shops and plenty of pedestrians using the shops.

Pedestrians are people on foot.

1 Label this photograph of a town centre using words from the box.

Taxis   Buses   Pedestrians   Tall buildings

2 Town centres provide many services for people. Match each service to what it is used for.

Services	What they are used for
Shops	Eating and drinking
Banks	Buying things
Cafes	Using the cash machine
Cinemas	Watching films

3 Traffic can cause problems in town centres. Use words from the car to fill the gaps in these sentences.

crooked   dirty   noisy   monkey   dangerous

Town centres are .... because of car engines and horns.

The air is .... because of car exhausts.

The roads are .... to cross because there are too many cars.

ACTIVITY:
1. Draw a picture of a town centre near where you live. Label the things your picture shows.
2. Write lists of the good and bad things about the town centre.

Investigating Traffic Problems

You can collect data (information) about traffic problems by counting cars or asking people questions. When you ask people questions you are doing a **survey**.

1 Decide if you would collect data about these things by counting or by using a survey. Circle your answers.

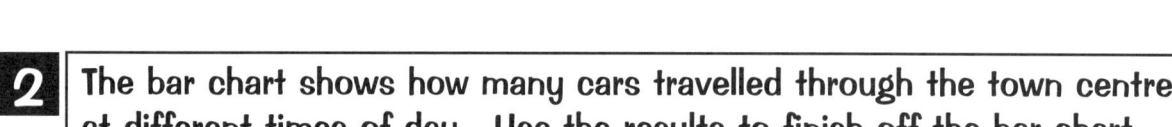

a) The number of cars in a car park. counting / survey
b) How shopkeepers feel about the number of cars. counting / survey
c) The amount of traffic on a road. counting / survey
d) How elderly people get into town each week. counting / survey

2 The bar chart shows how many cars travelled through the town centre at different times of day. Use the results to finish off the bar chart.

Results:	
Number of cars counted before lunch (10 am - 12 pm)	100
Number of cars counted after lunch (2 pm - 4 pm)	100

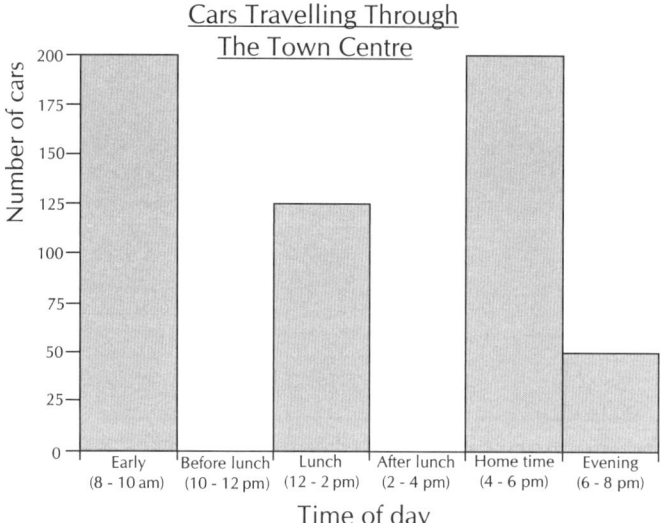

3 Use the bar chart to decide if these statements are true or false.

	True	False
There is most traffic early in the morning and at home time.	☐	☐
In the evening lots of cars drive through the town centre.	☐	☐
The amount of traffic goes up at lunchtime compared to before and after lunch.	☐	☐

ACTIVITY:
There would be less traffic if people used buses, walked or cycled instead of driving. Design a poster encouraging people to leave their car at home.

Section 2 — Local Traffic

Pedestrianising the Town Centre

Town centres can become noisy and dangerous. One solution is to cover the street with pavement and pedestrianise it. This means only people on foot are allowed in.

1 Colour in the area between the services on the High Street to show it has been pedestrianised.

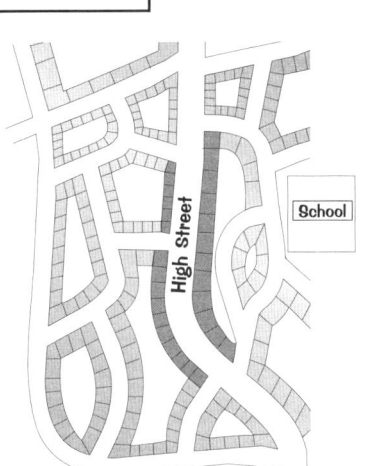

■ = Houses
■ = Services (shops, banks, etc.)
☐ = Pedestrianised area (only people on foot are allowed in)

Colour in the box in the key too.

2 Pedestrianisation doesn't solve all the problems because the traffic will just use different roads. Circle the correct words in these sentences.

Use the map to help you.

Now that the cars can't go through the High Street they have to **FLY OVER / GO ROUND THE EDGE OF** the town.
This could mean that more people would be driving past the school — this would be **DANGEROUS / NICE** for school children.
Also, the streets of houses will probably have **MORE / LESS** cars going past, which will make life **NOISIER / QUIETER** for residents.

3 Different people have different feelings about the pedestrianisation. Match up the people to how they feel about the pedestrianisation.

"My sales have gone down because fewer car drivers stop outside."

"It's much easier to buy things because you can walk from shop to shop."

"We have a lot more traffic on our street now as people park here instead of in town."

 Local resident    Shopper    Shopkeeper

Pedestrianisation might seem like the perfect solution — but cars will just go a different way.

Section 2 — Local Traffic

Constructing a Bypass

Bypasses are roads that are built round old villages or crowded town centres so that cars don't have to go through these places.

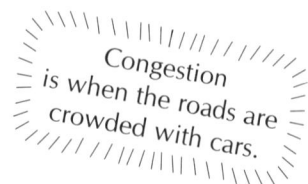
Congestion is when the roads are crowded with cars.

1 Match up each problem with how the bypass solved it.

| The traffic through the village was very noisy. | Cars could only move slowly through the village. | Cars caused congestion in the narrow village streets. |

The new bypass means traffic travels faster.   The new bypass can take a greater amount of traffic.   Less traffic means life is quieter for the village residents.

2 Some places are better than others to build bypasses. Use words from the road to fill in the gaps below.

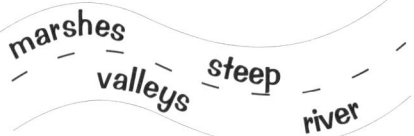
marshes valleys steep river

When bypasses are built, ... hills are avoided because it is expensive to construct roads over them. Often roads follow .... as they have a gentle slope. Wet .... are difficult to build roads on. .... banks are also a problem because they can flood.

3 Use phrases from the box to label the map of the new bypass.

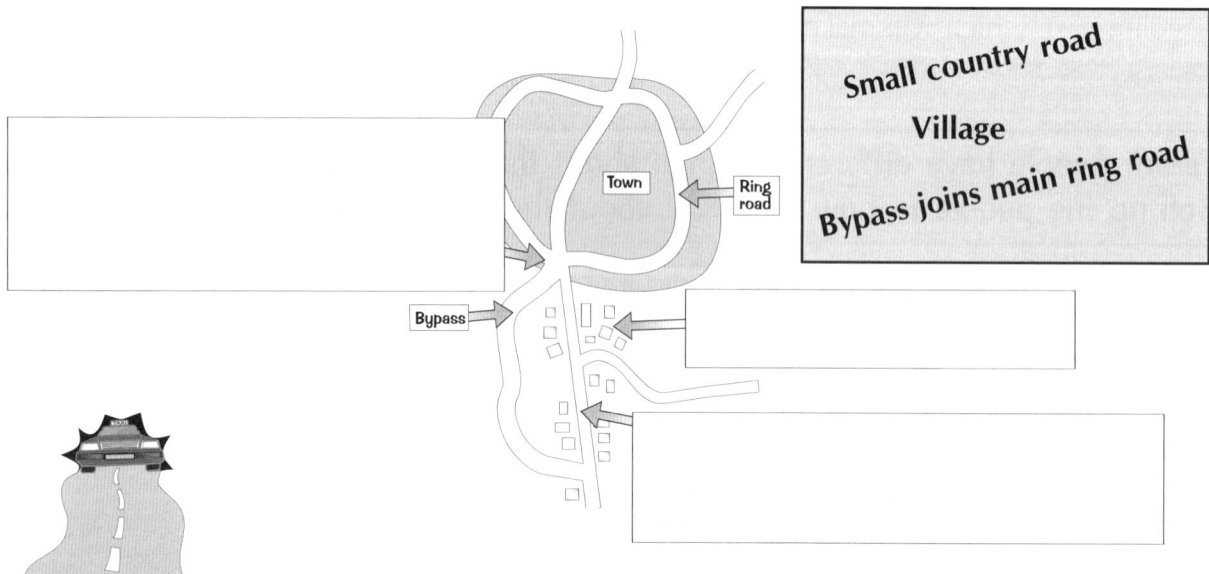

Small country road
Village
Bypass joins main ring road

Bypasses help traffic whizz past the town — not through the town.

Section 2 — Local Traffic

Understanding Different Opinions

Everyone thinks about things differently — everyone has different **opinions**.
When a bypass is built, some people feel it is a good idea, but others think it is a bad idea.

1 Label the different ways of letting other people know about our opinions.

Letters to the paper   Protests   Sitting in the corner sulking
Meetings   Surveys

2 How someone feels about something can depend on what they do and who they are. Match the speech bubbles to the people to show who said what.

"The bypass has cut across my land, so I have less space for crops."

"I can get to my office in the town much quicker now."

"Our village is much quieter now the bypass has been built."

3 Decide if the farmer and businessman above would think the bypass is a good or bad idea. Circle your answers.

        Farmer   good idea / bad idea

        Businessman   good idea / bad idea

ACTIVITY:
Imagine a bypass is being built near your school.
Write a letter to a newspaper explaining why you think it is a good or a bad idea.

Section 2 — Local Traffic

Does a Bypass Solve Problems?

When bypasses are built there are good and bad changes.

1 Tick the boxes to show if you think the changes caused by the bypass below are good or bad.

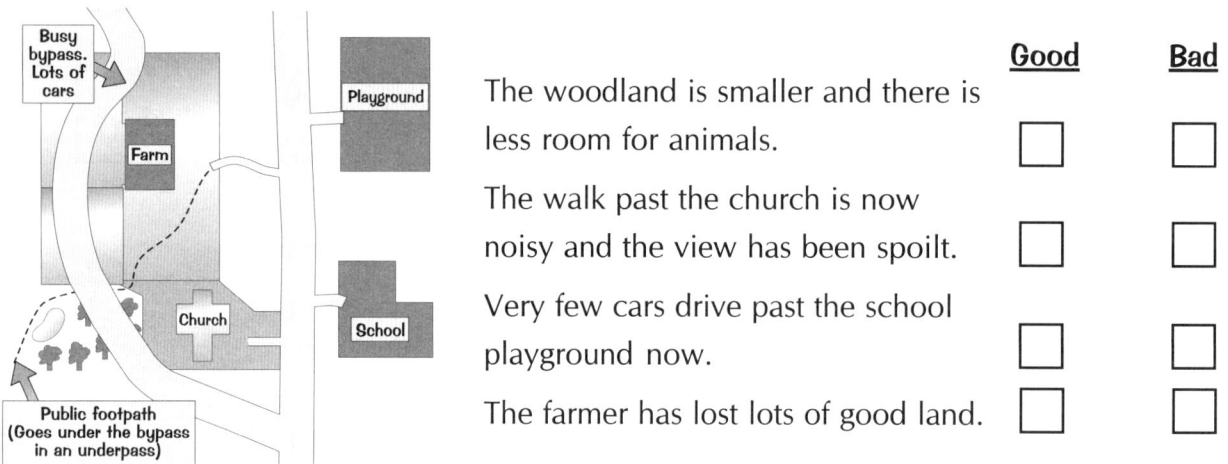

	Good	Bad
The woodland is smaller and there is less room for animals.	☐	☐
The walk past the church is now noisy and the view has been spoilt.	☐	☐
Very few cars drive past the school playground now.	☐	☐
The farmer has lost lots of good land.	☐	☐

2 Animals, such as birds, often suffer when a bypass is built. Use words from the box to fill in the gaps in the sentences.

> tarmac   grow   noisy   trees   sausages

Birds really lose out. People chop down our .... and we get a .... road covered in .... instead. Eventually things do get better when the new trees ....

3 People aren't always happy when bypasses are built either. Draw a happy or sad face to show how each person feels.

"The underpass is a smelly dark place."

"I can never get across the bypass on my tractor."

"Our church services are very noisy now."

Bypasses do have benefits, but they also cause BIG problems for some animals and people...

Section 2 — Local Traffic

Section 3 — A Seaside Town

Locating Llandudno

You can get to the seaside town of Llandudno by either rail or road — it depends on which you prefer and where you're coming from...

1 Look at the maps and circle the words that complete each sentence correctly.

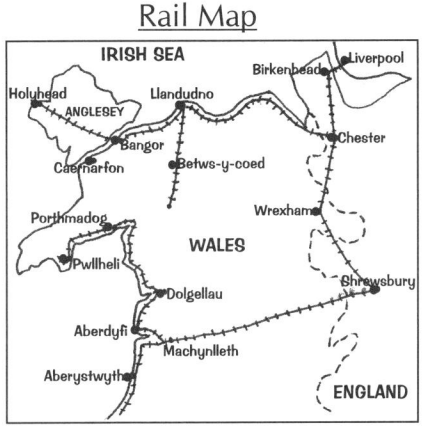

Rail Map

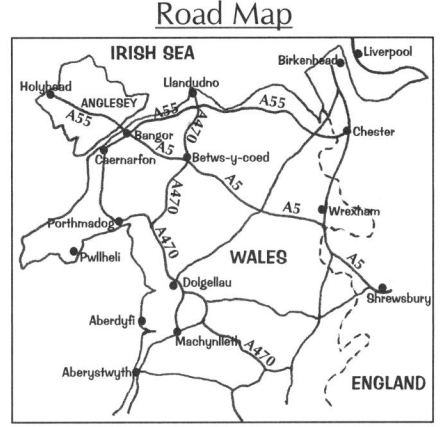

Road Map

Llandudno is **INLAND / AN ISLAND / BY THE COAST**.

Anglesey is **INLAND / AN ISLAND / A CITY**.

Chester is in **ENGLAND / WALES / THE IRISH SEA**.

2 Complete the sentences below using words from the signpost.

Use the maps in Q1 to help you.

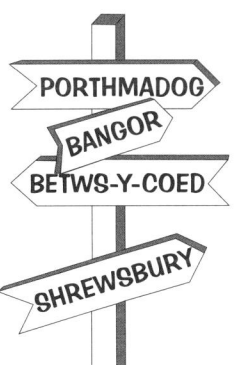

a) If someone from Caernarfon wanted to go by train to Llandudno, they'd have to get to .... first, which is the nearest station to Caernarfon.

b) From ...., it would be quicker to drive straight to Llandudno than go all the way around in a train.

c) If you were travelling to Llandudno by road from ...., you'd take the A5, changing onto the A470 at ....

3 Underline three reasons why some people might prefer taking trains to cars.

there's more privacy
can stop when you want
creates less pollution
can sit back and relax
might meet new people

ACTIVITY: Write about how you will get home tonight. What type of transport will you use? How long will it take? What places do you pass on the way? Who do you go with?

Features of a Seaside Town

Many people visit seaside towns because of their natural features.
But the features added by people who live there are important too.

1 Complete each sentence about the photos below using the words provided.

hills   rainforest   town

The .... and the beach are natural features of this landscape. Humans added to these natural features by building a ....

money   boats   fishing

The natural harbour allows many of the town's residents to earn their living by ....
They keep their .... in the harbour.

ice cream   tourists   sand

The sandy beach attracts lots of .... during the hot weather. One job for local people is selling .... to the tourists.

fairground   ranch   families

People have built a .... at this seaside town. This added leisure attraction makes seaside holidays more fun for ....

ACTIVITY: Imagine you are at the seaside. Write a postcard to tell your teacher all about the things you have seen and done. Don't forget to mention the weather.

Land Uses

A seaside town has to use its land for many different things, like houses, tourism and industry.

1 Look at the map below and make a tally chart of the way the land is used.

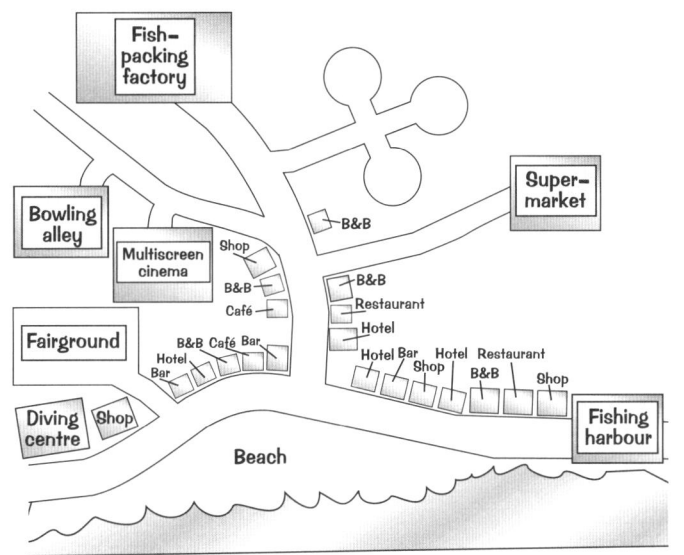

Tally up each different kind of facility shown on the map in the correct row in the table.

Then write the total in to show which activities need the most facilities.

ACTIVITY	TALLY	TOTAL
Accommodation hotels, B&Bs		
Food and Drink bars, restaurants, cafes		
Leisure places to have fun		
Shopping places to buy things		
Industry factories, fishing, etc.		

2 Circle the three buildings that would be used by both tourists <u>and</u> local residents.

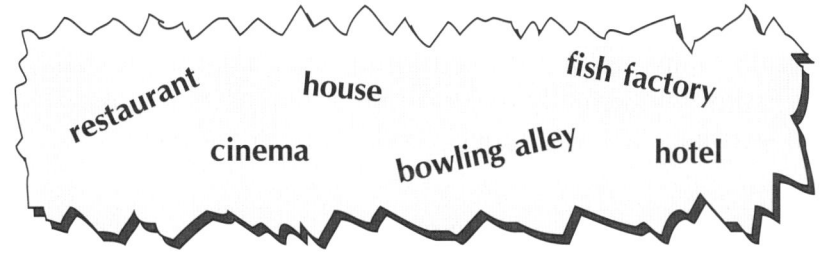

Not all coastal towns are tourist seaside towns — some are fishing villages or factory towns...

Section 3 — A Seaside Town

Economic Activity

People in a seaside town have to do things to earn money. This is called economic activity. A lot of it is to do with tourism but there are other jobs too.

1 Answer each riddle below by choosing the correct type of business.

I'm a small building near the beach with a big front window.
   I'm a ....
I'm a medium sized building with lots of rooms.
   I'm a ....
I'm a large building with hardly any windows and I smell.
   I'm a ....

Options: bed and breakfast, fish factory, shop

2 Match the sentences about the people below to their economic activities (jobs).

Mr Jones owns a boat — runs a restaurant
Mrs Kettle is very creative — catches fish
Mrs Little is a good cook — makes craftwork

3 There are often three stages in getting a product to the public — someone collects the material, someone makes something with it, and someone else sells it. Read about the people below and write their names in the boxes.

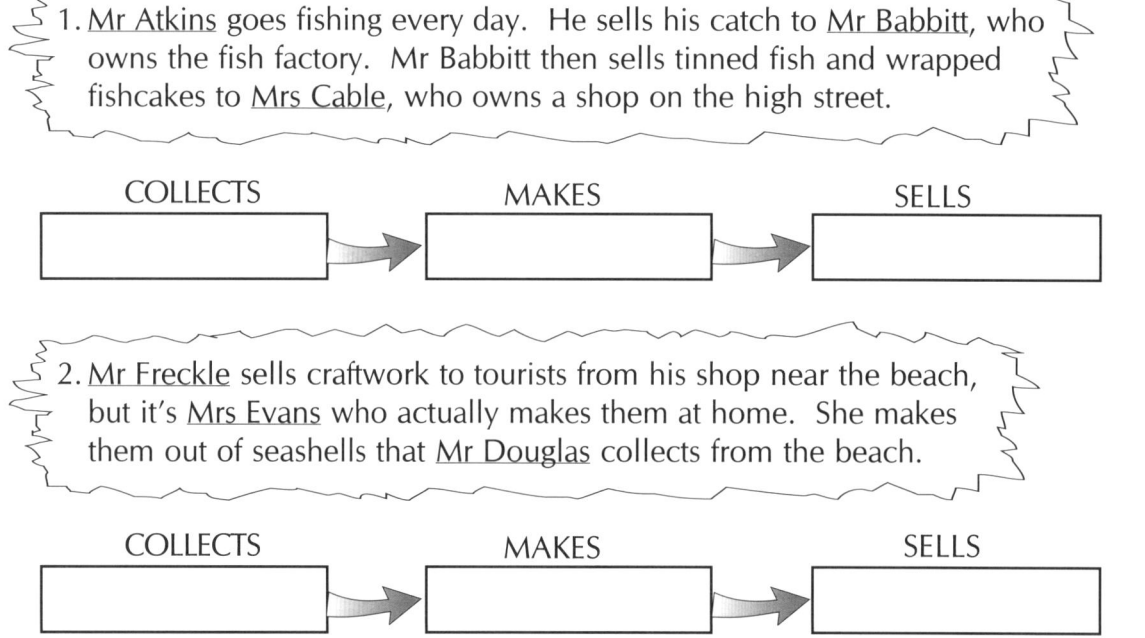

1. Mr Atkins goes fishing every day. He sells his catch to Mr Babbitt, who owns the fish factory. Mr Babbitt then sells tinned fish and wrapped fishcakes to Mrs Cable, who owns a shop on the high street.

COLLECTS → MAKES → SELLS

2. Mr Freckle sells craftwork to tourists from his shop near the beach, but it's Mrs Evans who actually makes them at home. She makes them out of seashells that Mr Douglas collects from the beach.

COLLECTS → MAKES → SELLS

It's surprising how many different jobs there are in a small seaside town.

Section 3 — A Seaside Town

Problems in a Seaside Town

It might seem like a dream to live in a pretty seaside town — but the things that make it so good can also cause problems...

1 Match up the problems caused by visitors with the part of the environment that gets harmed.

Visitors can harm the environment that they've come to enjoy.

visitors' cars cause air pollution — clean sea water for swimming
boats can cause water pollution — lots of open space
visitors leave litter on the beach — fresh air
tourism causes more buildings — peace and quiet
noisy crowds during tourist season — beautiful beaches

2 Put the places below into the correct lists to show how long they are probably open.

Hint: Think about whether tourists or local people or both use each place.

fairground, craft shop, post office, newsagent, supermarket, bed & breakfast

All Year Round	Tourist Season Only

3 What do locals in seaside towns do when the tourists have gone? Underline the correct endings to the sentences below.

a) Jennifer is a lifeguard at the beach in the tourist season.
   The rest of the year she **hibernates / teaches swimming at the local school**.

b) Ken fixes the rides at the fairground during the tourist season.
   The rest of the year he **fixes machinery for the local people / goes on the rides**.

c) Linda works at a bed & breakfast during the tourist season.
   The rest of the year she **talks to herself / works in the local fish factory**.

ACTIVITY: Make a list of all the things in your area that might attract tourists. Draw a picture of your favourite one from the list.

Section 3 — A Seaside Town

How Are Seaside Towns Different?

Seaside towns are different from inland towns in many ways — but they are similar in some ways too...

> Inland towns are towns that are not near the sea.

1 Look at the picture of a seaside town below and then cross out the wrong words in each sentence below.

Seaside Towns

In this picture, people are strolling on the road because **there is no traffic / the pavements smell**. Everybody seems **in a rush / relaxed** and many of them are probably **aliens / on holiday**.
On this street there are probably lots of little **shops / factories**.
Many seaside towns are **underneath / at the end of** roads, so it's **likely / unlikely** that visitors will have come specially and not because they're on their way to somewhere else.

2 Tick the sentence out of each pair which describes a seaside town instead of an inland town.

1. ☐ A lot of money comes from tourism ☐ A lot of money comes from factories
2. ☐ Local farmers have a market in town ☐ Local fishermen sell to hotels
3. ☐ Main roads lead to the centre of town ☐ Main roads lead to the beach
4. ☐ Sits between hills and the coast ☐ Spreads out into surrounding countryside
5. ☐ Same level of activity all year round ☐ Busier during summer

---

ACTIVITY: Make a poster to advertise a seaside town to tourists. Don't forget to mention all the things they can do there.

Section 3 — A Seaside Town

Section 4 — The Mountain Environment

Mountain Features

Mountain ranges are found in different parts of the planet — but all ranges are similar in many ways.

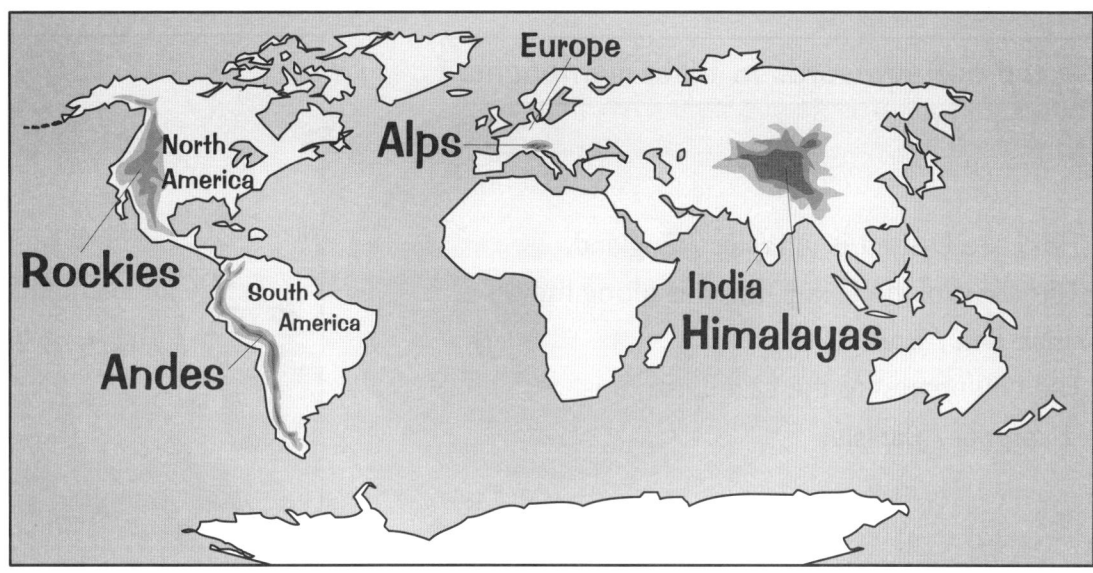

1 The map above shows some of the world's biggest mountain ranges. Write the names of the mountain ranges next to their descriptions.

This range stretches down the west coast of North America. ....

The world's longest mountain range is in South America. ....

The world's highest mountains are in the range just above India. ....

This range in the middle of Europe is great for skiing. ....

2 Circle the right words to complete the sentences about mountains.

The tops of mountains are so cold that there is often **SNOW / JELLY** there all year round.

Lower down on the slopes, **GRASS / HAIR** and trees grow.

The **VALLEYS / ROADS** between mountains often have soil that is good for **FARMING / EATING**.

Hills are **BIGGER / SMALLER** than mountains and their tops are often more **ROUNDED / JAGGED**.

ACTIVITY:
Use books to find out the name of the highest mountain in the world. Which country is it in? What other facts can you find out about it?

The Lake District

The Lake District is full of mountains, hills, valleys, lakes and rivers. The area attracts many visitors.

1 Circle the correct words in these sentences.

Use the map to help you.

a) The Lake District is in **Wales / England**.
b) The coast of the Lake District is along the **Irish Sea / North Sea**.
c) The city nearest to the Lake District is **Liverpool / Carlisle**.

The Lake District gets its name from the lakes between the mountains.

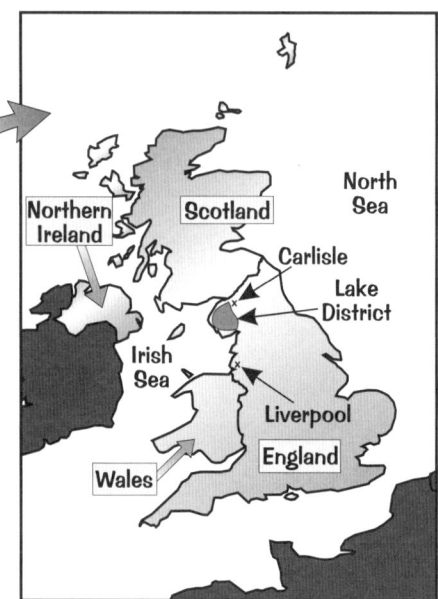

2 Use words from the box to label the photos of visitors enjoying activities in the Lake District.

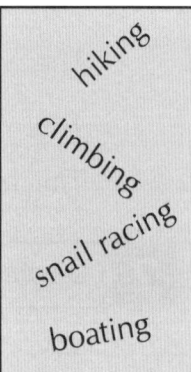

hiking climbing snail racing boating

3 Below are activities that people do in the Lake District. Underline the ones that are done on the lakes.

I say chaps, fancy a hike?

fishing   climbing   canoeing   water-skiing
hiking   swimming   shopping   sailing

A mountain environment is not just mountains — there are usually lakes and rivers too.

Section 4 — The Mountain Environment

Mountain Weather

Mountain weather mainly depends on height — the higher you go, the colder and windier it gets.

1 The bar graphs below show the temperature and rainfall of a mountain each month. Draw bars in the blank columns by using the information under the graphs.

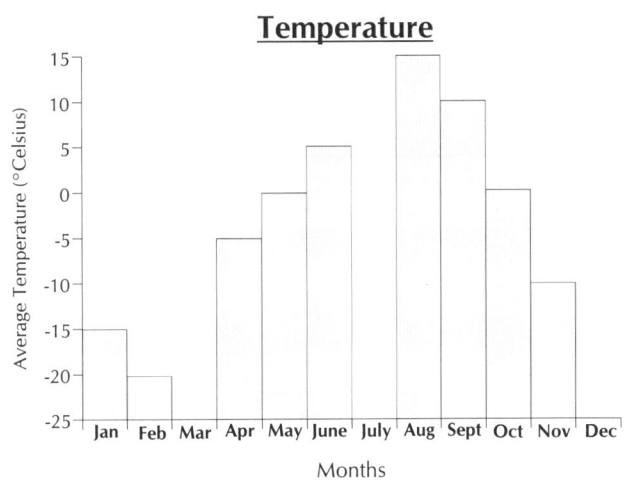

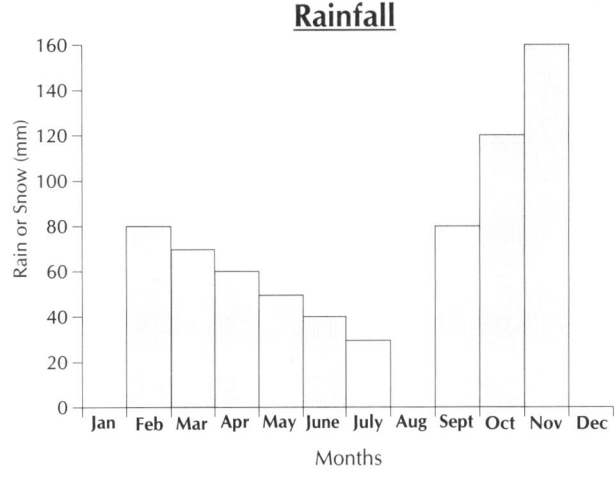

TEMPERATURE

It's 5 °C colder in March than it is in April.

It's 5 °C hotter in July than it is in June.

December is the same temperature as January.

RAINFALL

January is twice as wet as May.

August is half as wet as June.

December is twice as wet as April.

2 Fill in the gaps in this passage using words from the mountain.

Tall mountains have .... at the top all year round,

but snow is also found on the .... for much of the year.

Snowstorms are common during winter and the wind is

.... enough to move whole piles of fallen snow.

These .... can be deep enough to bury a person or even a house.

Sometimes masses of snow begin .... down the side of a mountain quickly.

These .... can be very dangerous for people in their paths.

Brrr....Mountain tops have the world's strongest winds and coldest temperatures.

Section 4 — The Mountain Environment

Weather and Tourism

On the tops of tall mountains, the snow never melts and nothing much grows. But people still enjoy using mountains for lots of activities.

1 The weather affects what activities you can do on mountains. Write these activities under the right kind of weather.

Rock-climbing   Skiing   Snowboarding   Hiking   Tobogganing

SNOWY WEATHER	FINE SUMMERY WEATHER

2 Cross out the wrong words in these sentences.

Ski resorts in mountains like the Alps attract people when there is lots of **(snow / rain)**. When the snow stops over the **(summer / winter)**, tourists stop going to the ski resorts and they are **(less busy / busier)**.

In the Lake District people do lots of **(walking / skiing)**. In bad, stormy weather, some people don't want to walk in the Lake District and there are **(fewer / more)** visitors.

3 Match the bits of writing to the holiday brochures they came from.

This is one of the most popular walking regions in the country. There is a huge choice of walks, for all levels, whether you like scrambling up mountainsides or wandering from village to village.

The Alps Holiday Brochure

Welcome to winter paradise! You'll love the beautiful scenery, warm hospitality and endless acres of snow!

The Lake District Holiday Brochure

ACTIVITY:
Design a holiday brochure page for the area where you live. You should include the good things about your area and the activities you can do there. Remember — you are trying to PERSUADE people to visit your area, not put them off.

Section 4 — The Mountain Environment

Effects of Tourism

Tourism is an important industry in mountainous areas. This can be good for local people, but it's not always good for the environment...

1 Tick the effects of tourism that are good for local people.

- ☐ There are more crowds in the local area.
- ☐ Local people can get jobs in resorts.
- ☐ There is more litter in the local area.
- ☐ Local restaurants and bars have plenty of customers.
- ☐ Local people can find jobs building resorts.
- ☐ Local people can sell craftwork to tourists.
- ☐ There is more pollution in the local area.

2 In mountain resort areas, local people can find a wide range of jobs. Underline the jobs which are important in mountain resorts.

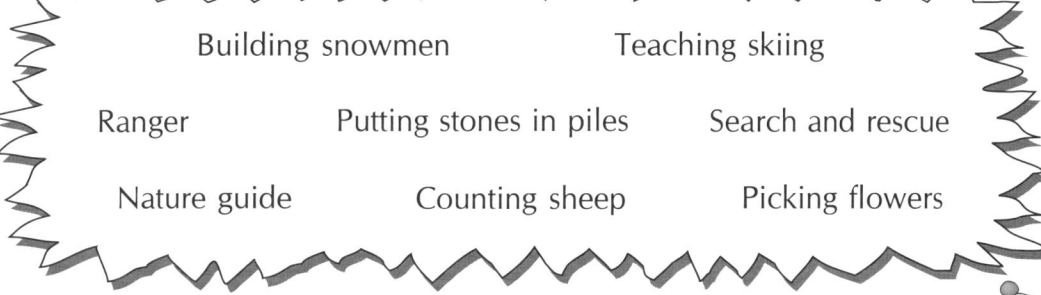

Building snowmen   Teaching skiing
Ranger   Putting stones in piles   Search and rescue
Nature guide   Counting sheep   Picking flowers

3 People must be careful not to damage the mountain environment. Shade in the activities which are BAD for the mountain environment.

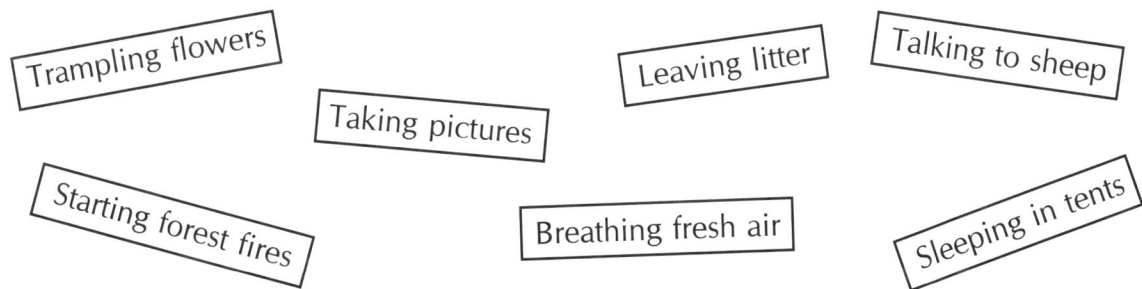

Trampling flowers   Leaving litter   Talking to sheep
Taking pictures
Starting forest fires   Breathing fresh air   Sleeping in tents

ACTIVITY:
Any environment can be spoilt if people don't know how to take care of it.
Write a list of rules people should follow to look after your school environment.
Think about different things that happen at school — like art lessons and lunch time.

Section 4 — The Mountain Environment

Planning a Holiday

Mountains can be dangerous places — so good planning and special equipment are needed for mountain holidays.

1 Different kinds of mountain holiday need different equipment. Under each picture of equipment, write the type of holiday it is for.

Skiing   Camping   Hiking   Climbing

....

2 All mountain holidays can be dangerous — but many dangers can be reduced. Match the dangers to the most sensible ways of reducing them.

Getting lost — Don't ski or climb beyond warning signs.

Starting an avalanche — Take care near rivers and lakes.

Suffering from injuries — Take enough food with you when hiking.

Starving to death — Bring a map and let people know where you're going.

Drowning — Wear the correct protective clothing.

3 The table below shows the weather conditions for a mountain resort. Use it to help you circle the best month for each type of mountain holiday.

Type of weather	Which months have this weather
SNOW	January, November, December
ICE	February
HEAVY RAIN	August, September
AVALANCHE WARNING	March, April
COOL AND SUNNY	May, June, October
WARM AND SUNNY	July

a) Skiing   **January / February**

b) Camping   **July / August**

c) Climbing   **September / October**

d) Hiking   **April / May**

What do you get if you cross a snowman and a shark? — Frostbite.

Section 4 — The Mountain Environment

Section 5 — Investigating Coasts

Rock Erosion

Erosion means 'wearing away'. Erosion shapes coastlines — waves wear away cliffs in certain places to make bays and headlands (land that sticks out into the sea).

1 Read the passage below, then label the photos using the words in bold.

CRASHING WAVES hit the cliffs and wear them away so that a **HEADLAND** is formed. Then waves crash into the headland to makes an **ARCH** that you can go through. Eventually the waves make the arch collapse and all that's left is the end of the arch, sticking up out of the water — this is called a **STACK**.

A

B

....

C

D

....

2 Label the photo below using the words from the box.

beach   stack   cliff

B)

C)

A)

It can take millions of years for waves to shape coastlines — you can't watch it happening.

Section 5 — Investigating Coasts

Headland Features on a Map

Ordnance Survey (OS) maps are detailed maps of the UK.
Unlike most maps, they show natural features like hills, cliffs and beaches.

1 Use the words from the box to complete the labels on the OS map.

.... are shaded yellowy-brown.

From above, ... are seen as lumps of rock in the sea.

beaches blue stacks

The sea is coloured ....

2 Look at the map and complete the sentences by circling the correct place names.

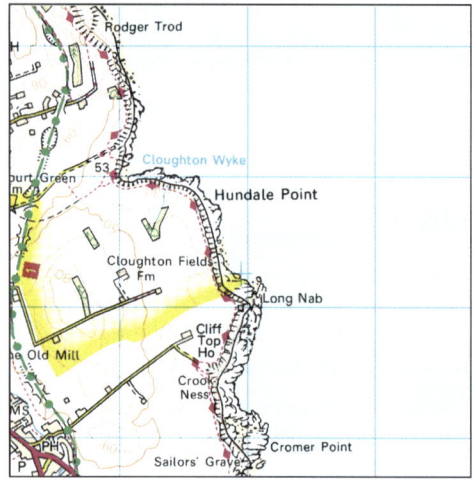

There is a long beach at **CROOK NESS / RODGER TROD**.
There is a stack near **SAILORS' GRAVE / RODGER TROD**.
(you'll need to look carefully for this one)

ACTIVITY: Use an OS map to find examples of:
    a) a place with a stack
    b) 3 different places with beaches
    c) something interesting (use the key to learn a new symbol)

Section 5 — Investigating Coasts

Human Activity

It's not only waves that cause erosion — human activity on cliff tops can wear away the land and make the cliffs crumble.

1 Tick the activity below that would cause the most erosion to a cliff top.

☐ walking along a cliff top
☐ digging a rock quarry on a cliff top
☐ building a house on a cliff top

All of these activities would cause some erosion to a cliff top.

2 Write the words below into the spaces to show how humans can cause cliffs to fall into the sea.

*crack   hotel   cliff   unstable   fall
     digging*

To build a large structure like a ...., you first have to lay a foundation. This means .... into the ground to create a basement. If you don't do this, the building might .... over. If you dig a foundation into the rock near a .... top, you could cause the rock to .... This crack could spread and before you know it, the whole cliff becomes ....

3 Tick the things that might cause a landslide if they were built on a cliff.

☐ a public garden   ☐ a fairground
☐ a resort hotel   ☐ a nature reserve
☐ a landscaped park   ☐ a supermarket

Plants help stop the soil on cliff slopes from sliding into the sea, so removing plants from cliff slopes can cause landslides.

A building on a cliff with a sea view sounds lovely, but it could one day end up in the sea...

Section 5 — Investigating Coasts

Beaches

Beaches can be made of sand, or small stones called shingle.
Beaches are created by the waves that crash against the rocks.

1 Put the letter of each sentence under its drawing, to show how waves slowly break rocks into sand.

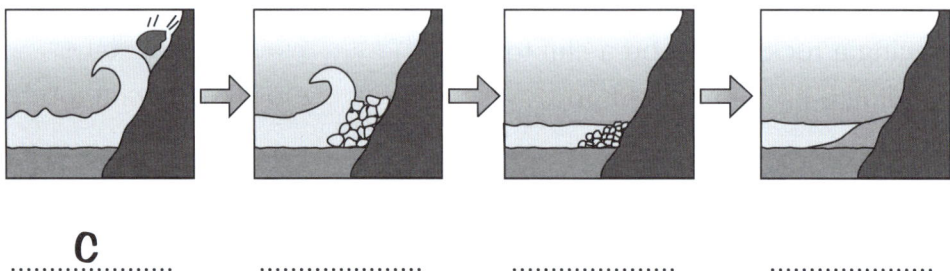

C ....

A Large pebbles are made as the rocks are worn down or broken by the waves.
B In time, the shingle erodes through wear and tear and eventually becomes sand.
C Rocks are broken off cliffs and boulders by the crashing waves.
D Shingle is created as the waves wear down the large pebbles into smaller ones.

2 On the OS map below, draw a ring round the part of the beach that you think is shingle.

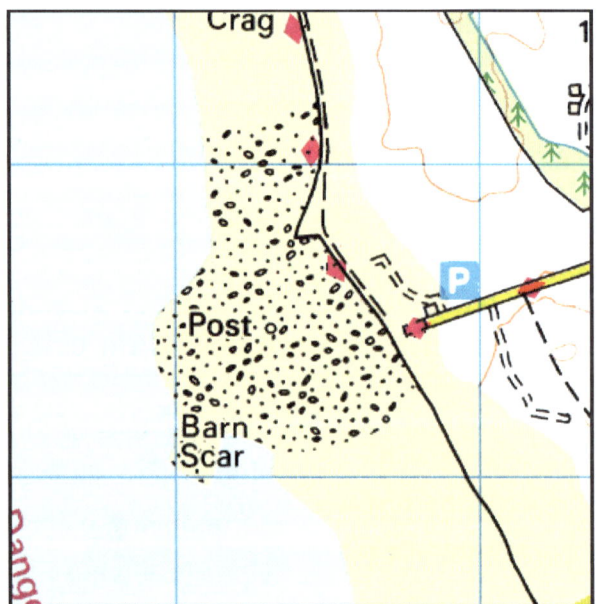

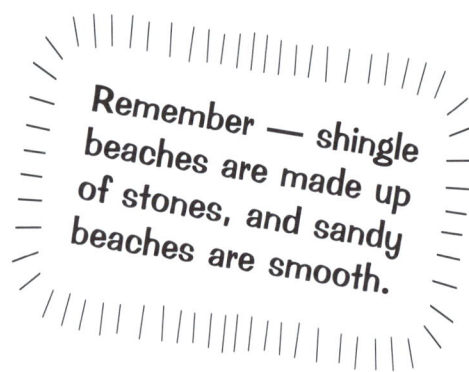

Remember — shingle beaches are made up of stones, and sandy beaches are smooth.

Sand and shingle beaches are both made of broken down and eroded rocks from the cliffs.

Section 5 — Investigating Coasts

Coastal Holidays

Different parts of the coast have different features, like cliffs or beaches or marshes. This affects the types of coastal holidays on offer.

1 Decide which map goes with which brochure. Write the correct letter in the space below the brochure.

SCARY DROP HOTEL
Situated in one of the most scenic spots in the region, we offer spectacular views of the rugged coastline and the sea beyond. There's walking and cycling and, for the more adventurous, rock climbing.

....

SNOOZY PLACE HOTEL
Laze in the sunshine on our sandy beach while the kids build sandcastles. Swim and body-surf in the sea. Discover the flowering sea poppies and prickly sea urchins out on the shingles. A perfect day!

....

SOGGY NEST HOTEL
If you think holidays are for the birds, then this is the place for you! Everything from warblers to waders come to feed and roost on our marshlands all year round. Bring your binoculars — you won't want to miss a thing!

....

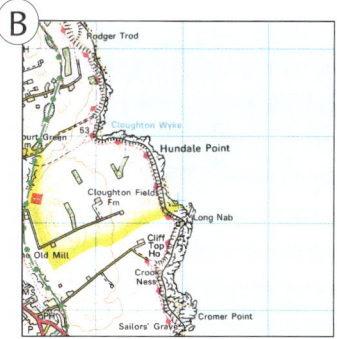
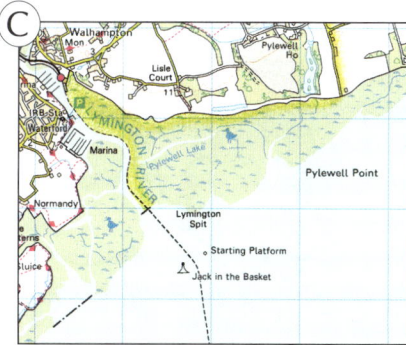

2 Match up the types of holiday-maker with the correct type of coastline.

- A sunbather — A coast with rugged cliffs
- A birdwatcher — A beach resort
- A cliff walker — A coastal marshland bird sanctuary

ACTIVITY: Use an OS map to find 3 places where you could go birdwatching.

Section 5 — Investigating Coasts

Coastal Land Uses

People living on the coast and people visiting the coast use the land for different things.

1 Tick the activities that could be done in and around the town on the map.

Use the key to help you.

a) visit a theme park
b) take pictures of a stack
c) have a walk in a park
d) go birdwatching on the marshes
e) visit a leisure centre
f) go to school
g) camp beside the beach

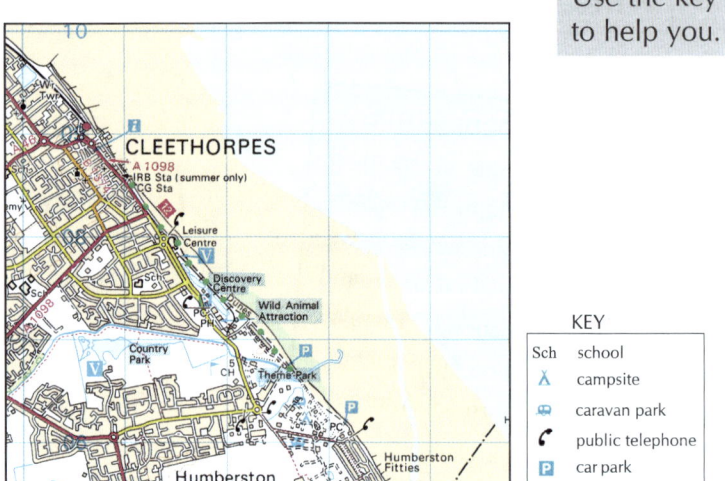

KEY
Sch — school
⋏ — campsite
— caravan park
✆ — public telephone
P — car park

2 Underline the places below that are mainly used for leisure.

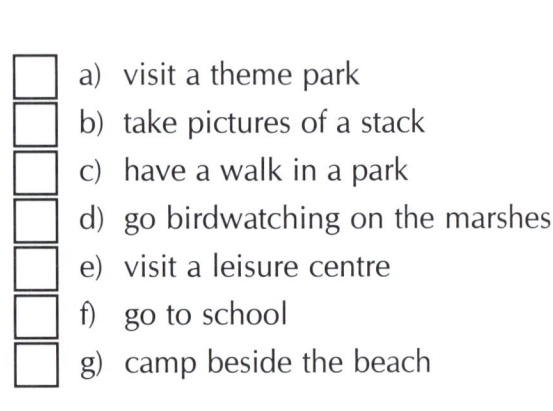

beach · train station · school · sports centre · golf course · church

Coastal land is used for both leisure activities and housing.

3 Match the attractions to the places where they might be found on the map.

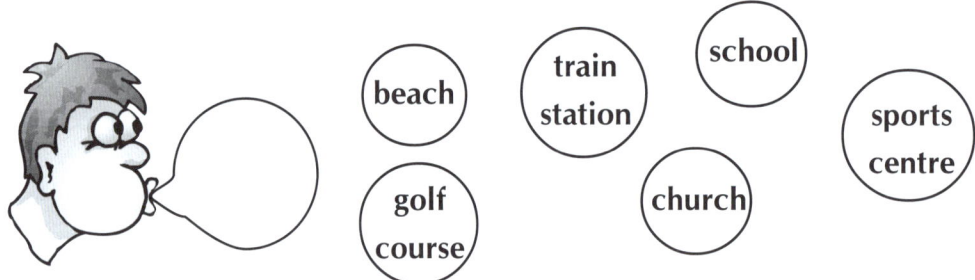

lions and bears — Country Park
outdoor pond — Discovery Centre
indoor swimming pool — Wild Animal Attraction
science exhibit — Leisure Centre

ACTIVITY: Make a list of the leisure activities you can do in the town on the map. Then make a list of the leisure activities you can do in your town. Which town would be the most fun to live in?

Protecting the Coastline

Human activity (like building houses) and natural activity (like weather and waves) cause the coastline to slowly fall into the sea. We can stop this from happening using some special methods...

1 Match the problems below to the best ways of protecting against them.

Problems   Protection Methods

Houses are flooded by waves   Cliff-face armouring makes cliff
every time there's a storm.   faces stronger.

The cliffs are weak and   Groynes (little walls) stop waves
crumble easily.   sweeping sand sideways along a beach.

The sand on the beach is   A breakwater stops waves from
slowly disappearing.   crashing so hard onto cliffs.

The crashing waves are   Sea walls stop waves from splashing
wearing away the cliffs.   onto and flooding streets.

A sea wall needs to be really strong, and is usually made of lots of stones.

2 Tick the two sentences that describe real ways of making a sea wall stronger.

☐ a) Use wire mesh to keep the stones in place when they're pounded by waves.

☐ b) Stick wads of chewing gum between the stones to keep them stuck together.

☐ c) Cover it in plastic sheeting to keep the stones from falling away.

☐ d) Put up a sign with a big hand on so the waves will know to stop before hitting it.

ACTIVITY: Design a poster to tell people about how we can stop the coastline falling into the sea. Remember to use lots of colour to make it eye-catching.

Section 5 — Investigating Coasts

Understanding Different Opinions

Below is a picture of a beautiful seaside village, and beside it are plans for how to change it. The villagers have to decide whether to change it or to keep it the same...

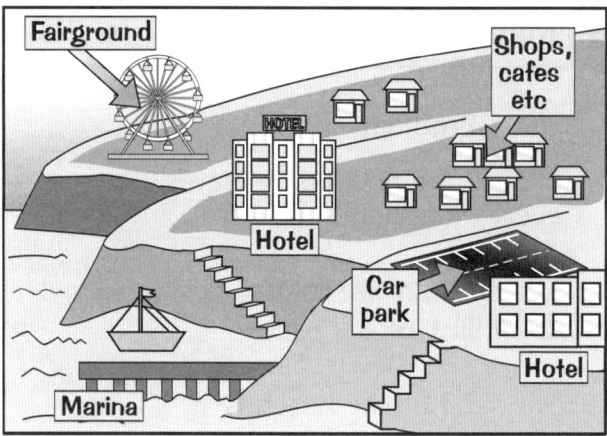

1 Match up the beginnings and ends of the sentences to show some reasons why the villagers don't want these changes.

Cutting steps into the cliffs could make   water, air and noise pollution.

Using boats in the bay would create   break up the close community.

Turning the village homes into shops would   spoil the beautiful scenery.

Putting up so many new buildings would   the cliffs crumble into the sea.

2 Changing this quiet seaside village wouldn't be all bad. Tick the good things.

☐ more people can enjoy the seaside   ☐ more fun attractions for local people

☐ more traffic causing air pollution   ☐ more litter in town and on beaches

☐ more jobs and money for local people   ☐ more people to become friends with

There are no perfect solutions to how land is used, but it's important that everyone gets their say.

Section 5 — Investigating Coasts

Section 6 — Passport to the World

Identifying Countries

There are hundreds of countries in the world of all shapes and sizes.
They all have different features that make them special.

1 You can learn to recognise a country from its shape. Write the letters of the country shapes next to the matching descriptions below.

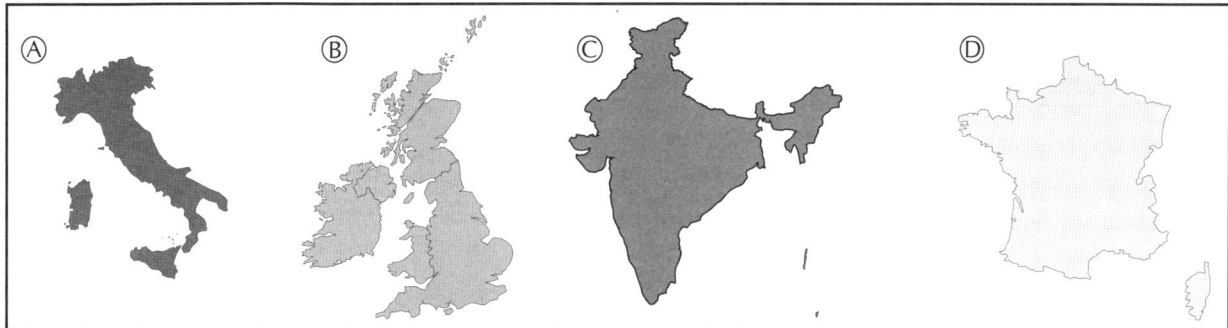

India looks like a triangle or arrow pointing downwards. ....

Italy looks like a leg or a high-heeled boot. ....

France is kind of square, or like a knight's shield. ....

The UK is two islands. The smaller island looks like a sideways face.
The larger island looks very hard to draw. ....

2 Draw lines to match up the foods to the countries they come from.

Haggis	Italy
Curry	France
Pizza	India
Baguette	Scotland

3 Unscramble the muddled words to find out where the postcards were sent from.

We've seen lions and giraffes on safari in **YEKAN**.

Here's me by the Leaning Tower of Pisa in **TILYA**.

We're in **RENCAF** and I've seen the Eiffel Tower in Paris.

I've seen kangaroos and koala bears in **ILASATURA**.

ACTIVITY:
Look in an atlas at the shapes of countries. Do any of them look like objects?
Pick five interesting countries and describe their shapes.
Swap with the person next to you and see if you can identify each other's countries.

Choosing a Holiday

People go all over the world for their holidays — where they go depends on what they like doing.

1 Sam asked 20 people, "Where is your favourite holiday place?" Use his results to complete the bar chart.

Sam's results table

Favourite Holiday Place	Number of People
Spain	5
USA	5
France	3
Italy	2
UK	1
India	1
Kenya	1
Australia	1
Switzerland	1

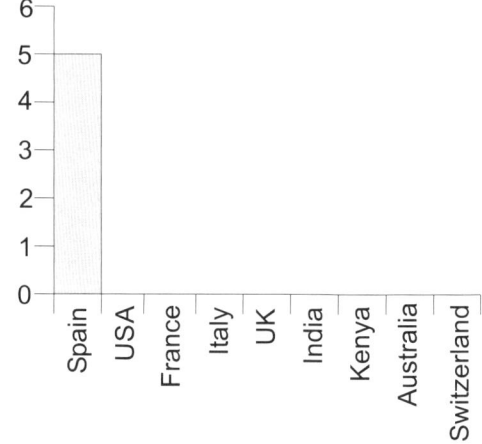

2 Circle the two most popular places. Then answer the questions below.

Spain   Morocco   Italy   USA   Switzerland

a) How many people in total chose these two places?   ....

b) Was this ¼, ½ or ¾ of all the people asked?   ....

3 Sam also asked the 20 people why they liked their favourite holiday place. The information he found out is in the table.

Reasons for Choosing the Place	Number of People
Warm, sunny weather	11
The beach	3
Doesn't take long to get there	2
It's different from the UK	2
Friends and family are there	1
Skiing	1

Use the information in the table and words from the car to fill in the gaps in these sentences.

Most people chose their favourite place because of the .... weather.

The second most important reason was the ....

Some people chose their favourite holiday place because it was .... the UK.

One person chose their holiday place because of the ....

The UK isn't very warm — so people often like to go to hot, sunny places on holiday.

Weather Across the World

The weather is very different across the world — no two places have exactly the same weather.

1 People in different places in the world said these things about their weather. Use this information to circle the right words in the sentences below.

- Farmers in Ethiopia are worried because there has been no rain for months.
- Parts of the USA were hit by snowstorms today.
- It's cold and pouring with rain here in Norway.
- Holidaymakers in Spain are enjoying warm, sunny weather.
- There is deep snow in Switzerland.

The two places which had snow are **ETHIOPIA / SWITZERLAND** and **NORWAY / THE USA**.

It was cold and wet in **NORWAY / SPAIN**.

The **COLD / DRY** weather was a problem in Ethiopia.

The weather was very good for holidays in **NORWAY / SPAIN**.

2 Kate went to Italy for a week. Use her diary of the weather to answer the questions below.

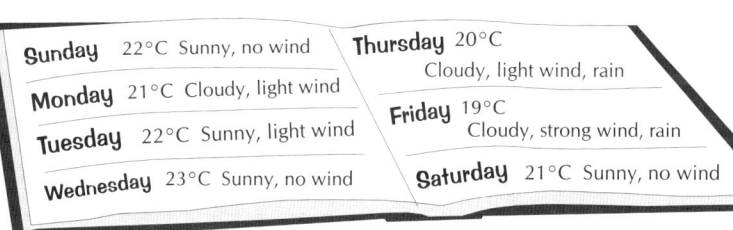

Sunday 22°C Sunny, no wind
Monday 21°C Cloudy, light wind
Tuesday 22°C Sunny, light wind
Wednesday 23°C Sunny, no wind
Thursday 20°C Cloudy, light wind, rain
Friday 19°C Cloudy, strong wind, rain
Saturday 21°C Sunny, no wind

a) Fill in each day's temperature in this chart. It has been started for you.

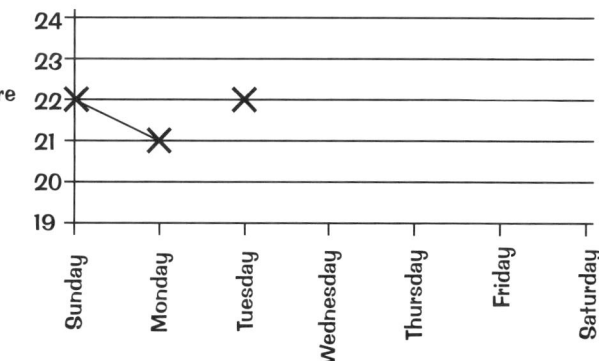

b) Draw a sunshine symbol like this (☼) in the right boxes, to show which days were sunny.

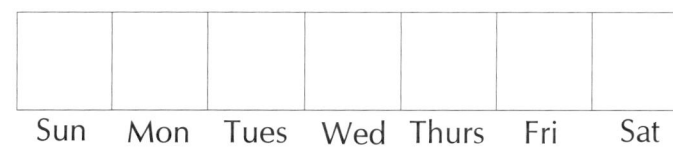

Sun Mon Tues Wed Thurs Fri Sat

c) Which was the windiest day? ....

d) How many days were rainy? ....

ACTIVITY:
Write a paragraph about the worst weather you can remember.
What did it feel like? How did it affect you and your family? How long did it last?

Section 6 — Passport to the World

Places in the News

The news tells us up-to-date stories about people and places from all over the world.

1 Match each headline to the reason why the story was in the news.

MANY PEOPLE DIE IN AN EARTHQUAKE IN INDIA.   It was about a famous person.

MISSING LOCAL SCHOOLGIRL IS FOUND SAFE AND WELL.   It was about a sporting achievement.

AUSTRALIAN SETS NEW WORLD SWIMMING RECORD.   It was a scary event and people died.

THE PRESIDENT OF THE USA VISITED GLASGOW TODAY.   It was a story that had a happy ending.

2 We can find out about different places from TV programmes. Match the programmes with the things they tell us about.

How to get to places and what they are like.

 A Look at Mexico City

 Life with the Inuits

 The News

 Fab Holidays

What's happening in the world right now?

Where do they live? What do they eat?

What jobs do people do here? What does the city look like?

3 These news stories are about Ethiopia (in Africa), and the UK. Some things in both stories are similar, and some things are different.

> Farmers in Ethiopia are struggling to stay alive. Crops are dying because there has been no rain for months. One farmer told us that he had tried to sow his food seeds three times, and each time they had shrivelled up. "I don't know how I can feed my family," he said, "I have no money at all".

> UK shops were busier than ever today as people ignored pouring rain in their rush to buy Christmas presents and food. Thousands of pounds were spent on turkeys, pies, chocolates and drinks in Scoffalot's supermarkets, and Zappit's stores said they had sold out of computer games.

Circle the correct words to complete the sentences.

Things that are similar

Both stories tell us about the **WEATHER / SHOPS** in the country.

The people in both countries need **COMPUTER GAMES / FOOD** to stay alive.

Things that are different

Ethiopia is very **POOR / SOGGY** while the UK is rich.

Ethiopia has **SNOWY / SUNNY** weather, while the UK is often rainy.

In Ethiopia people are dying of **COLD / STARVATION**, while in the UK people often eat too much.

News stories and TV programmes tell us about other people's lives in faraway places.

Section 7 — Geography, Maps and Numbers

OS Map for Reference

Use the map on this page to answer some of the questions in Section 7.

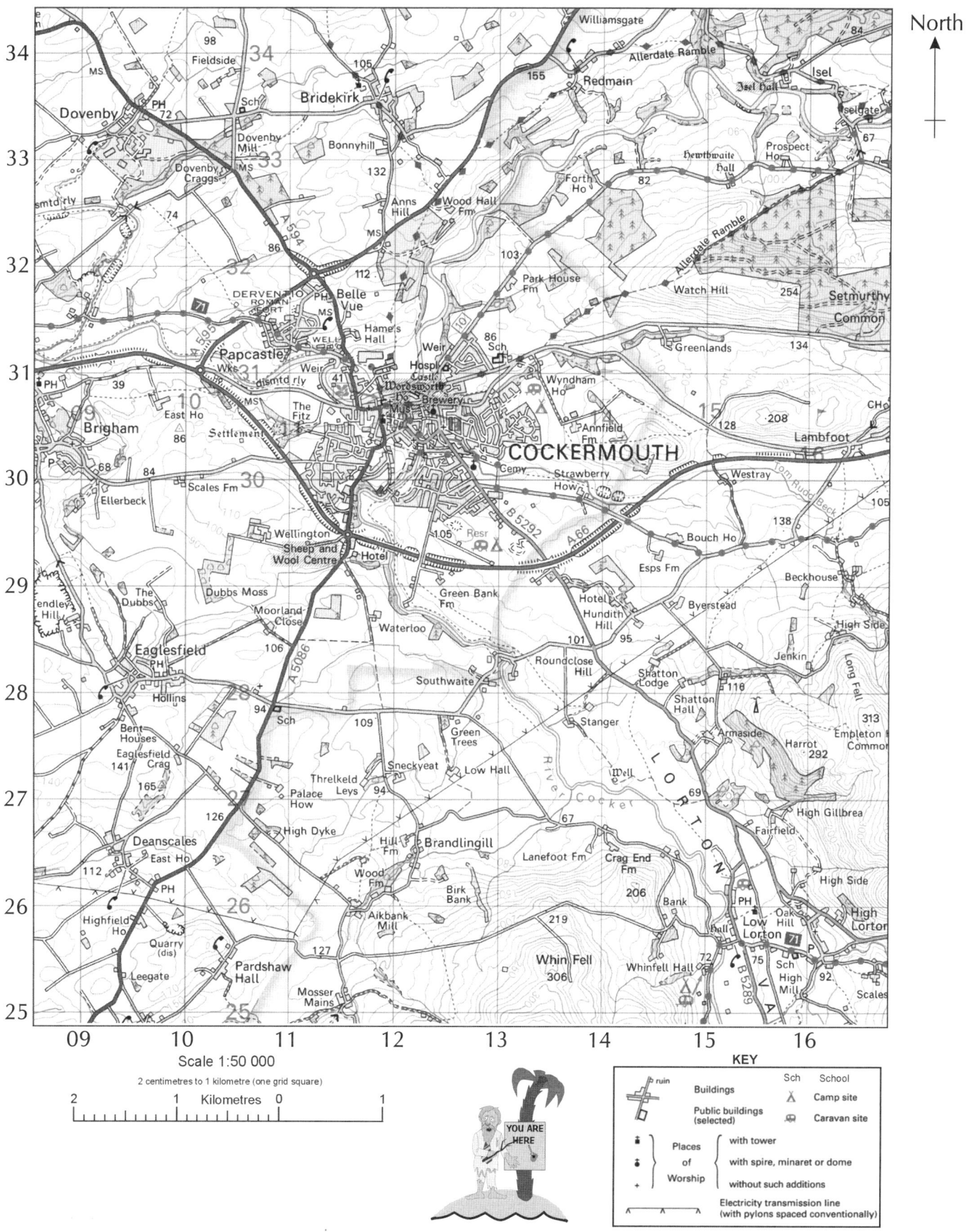

Maps are drawings of places as if they're seen from the air — and very useful they are too.

Reading Maps

A map's key unlocks the meaning of the map. It explains the symbols (pictures), lines, words and numbers.

1 Use the map of Cockermouth and its key on page 37 to help you write YES or NO next to each sentence.

   a) The biggest town on the map is Bridekirk. ....
   b) There are camping and caravan sites on the edge of the town of Cockermouth. ....
   c) There are more than two places of worship in the town of Cockermouth. ....

2 Use the Cockermouth map and key again to help you complete these sentences. Use words from the cloud.

   a) When I drive to Dovenby from Cockermouth, I use the .... road.
   b) The bus journey along the B5292 from Cockermouth to Low .... takes us under the .... road.

Cloud: M1, A594, Lorton, A66, Heylan

3 Tom lives in Toronto Avenue (top left of the map below). He walks to the park. Circle the correct words to describe how he gets there.

First I go along Toronto Avenue and walk into **Knights Road / Knox Street**.
Then I turn **right / left** into **Maximin Road / College Green**.
Then I have to cross **Bertha Road / Tollgate Road** to get into the park.

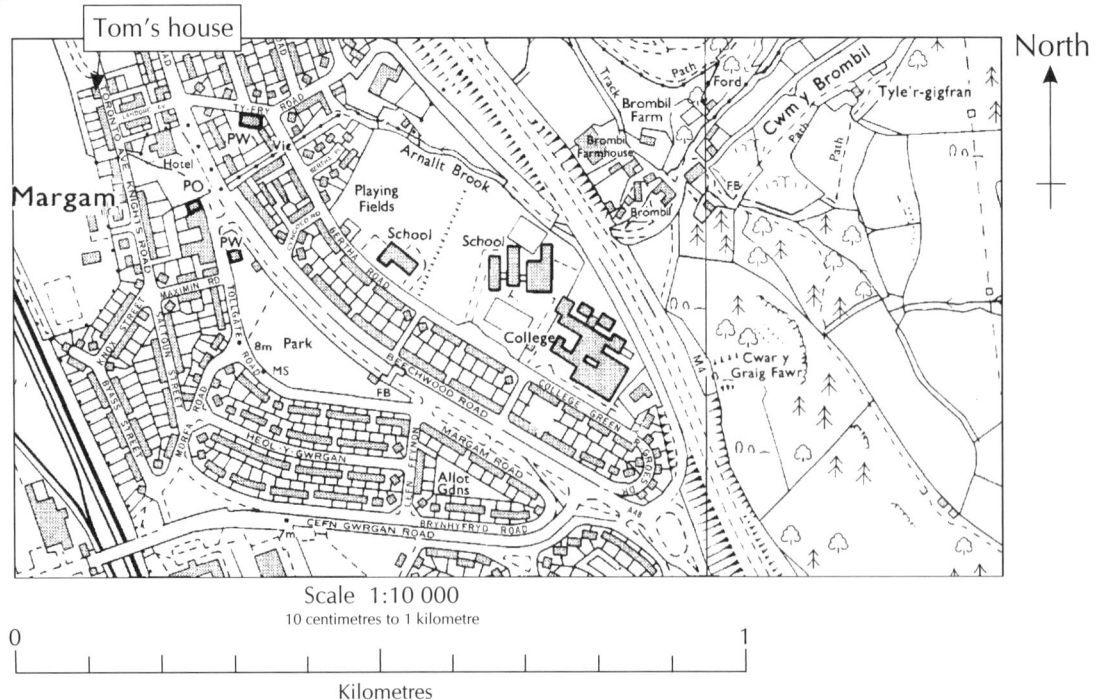

Scale 1:10 000
10 centimetres to 1 kilometre
0 — Kilometres — 1

Maps help you find out what's in a place and how to get there.

Section 7 — Geography, Maps and Numbers

Map Scales

The scale of a map allows you to work out how big or how far away places on the map are in real life.

1 Circle the correct words in the passage below about the map of Margam on page 38.

The map shows Margam a lot **SMALLER / BIGGER** than it really is. This is to make it fit on a **FOOTBALL PITCH / PIECE OF PAPER**. The **SCALE / MENU** tells us exactly how far in real life a distance on a map is. On this map, if a road is 10 centimetres long, it will really be **ONE KILOMETRE / TEN KILOMETRES** long.

2 Find the college on the Margam map and measure it with a ruler. Use the scale to answer the questions below with YES or NO.

a) The length of the college is more than 5 cm on the map. ....

b) The length of the college is about 1 cm on the map. ....

c) In real life, the college building measures about 1/10 of a kilometre (100 m) ....

3 Look at the Cockermouth map on page 37, which has a different scale. Choose numbers from the right to fill in the spaces in the sentences.

a) Jackie walked from the pub (symbol PH) in Eaglesfield (in square 0928) along the road until she came to the A5086 road. This distance on the map is .... cm, which is .... kilometres in real life.

You'll need a ruler to measure the distances.

b) The same day, Ian took a bus from Cockermouth to Dovenby. On the map, this journey is about 6 cm, which means the journey was about .... km long.

1   0.5
2.5   20
3   3000
1.25   1000

ACTIVITY:
Draw and label a map of your classroom. Remember to draw things as they would look if you were a spider looking down from the ceiling. The things that are bigger in real life should be bigger on your map.

Section 7 — Geography, Maps and Numbers

Compass Directions and Coordinates

A map is very useful, but without compass directions and coordinates, we wouldn't be able to tell each other where things are.

1 Fill in the missing four points of the compass.

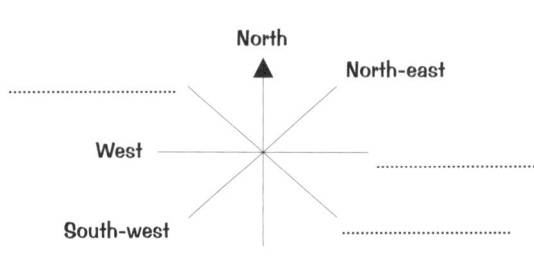

2 Complete the sentences by circling the correct word or phrase. Use the map of Cockermouth and its key on page 37.

a) There are lots of woods to the **NORTH-EAST / SOUTH-WEST** of Cockermouth.

b) The A66 main road goes roughly from **NORTH TO SOUTH / EAST TO WEST**.

c) There is a line of electricity pylons to the **SOUTH / NORTH** of Cockermouth.

3 The numbers on maps are called coordinates — they help us find places. Answer the questions about the Cockermouth map.

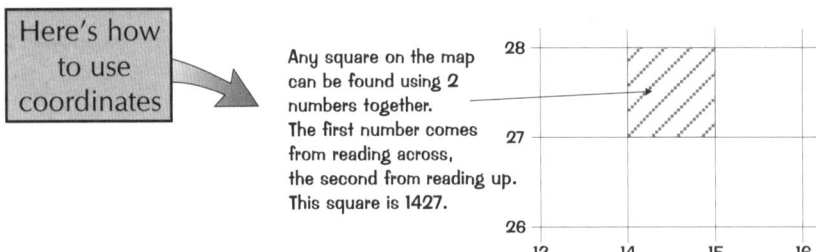

a) Name the hill in square 1325.

W......N FE......

b) Name the village in square 0933.

DO........BY.

4 You can fix an exact spot on a map by using 6-figure coordinates instead of 4. Circle the answers to the questions about the Cockermouth map.

Imagine each square is divided up even more. To find A's first three numbers, read across on the big scale — 11, then across on the mini-scale — 5. Do the same reading up to get the last three numbers.
A is at 115335.
The church is at 117337.

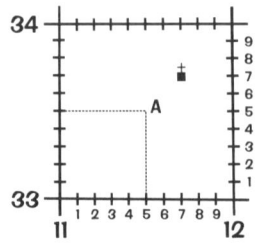

a) What feature is at 105335?

A CHIP SHOP / A SCHOOL.

b) What is there at 128301?

A PLACE OF WORSHIP / A ROCKET LAUNCH SITE.

ACTIVITY:
Find a feature on the Cockermouth map and give your partner its 4-figure coordinate. Your partner has to work out what the feature is. Then you should swap over. If you can do this, have a go with 6-figure coordinates.

Section 7 — Geography, Maps and Numbers

Populations

This page is all about the numbers of people (the 'population') in two places.

1 The table shows the populations of two places, Frogstop and Toadham. Add up the total populations for Frogstop and Toadham.

	Frogstop	Toadham
Children, aged 0 - 14 years	500	5 000
Young / middle-aged, 15 - 64 years	2 000	25 000
Elderly, aged 65 and over	2 500	20 000
TOTAL	....	....

2 Use the table above to match the beginnings of the sentences with their endings.

Toadham is   probably a village
Frogstop is   the most children
Toadham has   the fewest children
Frogstop has   probably a town

3 Complete the bar chart to show the population of each place. Use the table in Q1 to help you.

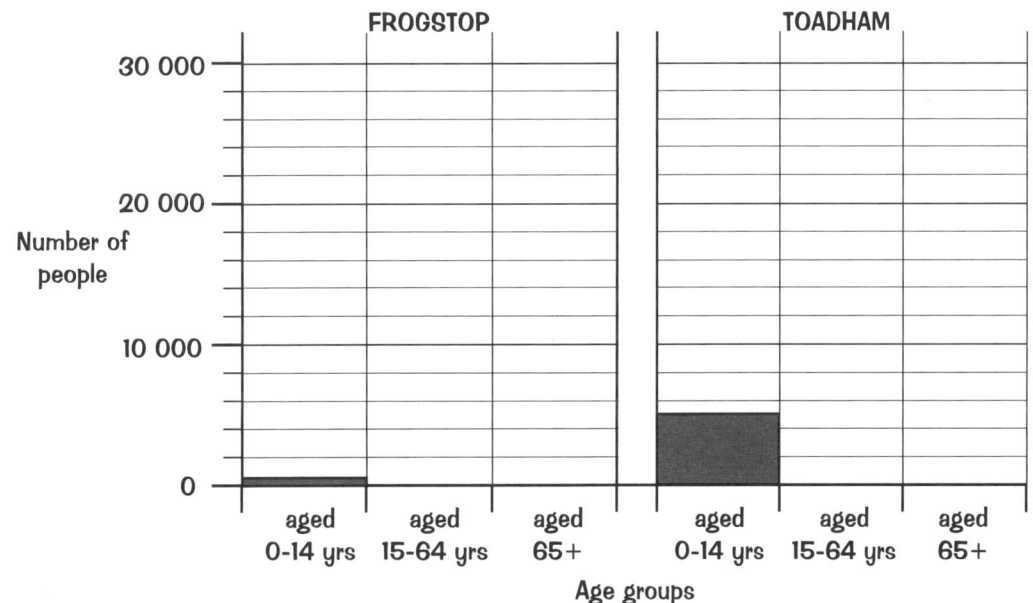

Phew! All these numbers make your head spin.

Section 7 — Geography, Maps and Numbers

The Answers

Section 1 — Water

Page 1

Q1 Deserts are coloured YELLOW.
Mountains are coloured GREY.
Oceans, lakes and rivers are coloured BLUE.

Q2 In order, the correct words are: oceans; salty; frozen; rain.

Q3 Moving water: river; stream.
Standing water: lake; reservoir; pond.

Page 2

Q1

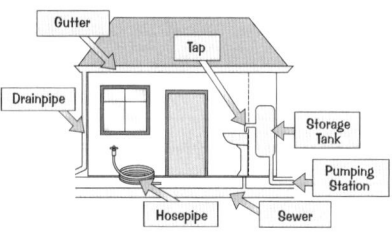

Q2 'Pump water in through pipes' should be ticked.

Page 3

Q1 cooking; drinking

Q2 Home — cooking rice
Leisure — swimming
Farming — watering crops
Industry — steam engine

Q3 In order, the missing words are: laundry; dishes; mopped; washed; watered; cooked; shower.

Page 4

Q1 In order, the missing words are: kettle; plants; clothes; shower; pipes.

Q2 a) and d) should be ticked.

Q3 energy; land

Page 5

Q1 Green coloured with green slime floating on top. Smells very bad. — Very bad to drink.
Clear. Doesn't smell of anything. — Good to drink.
Muddy and unclear. Doesn't smell. — Not very good to drink.

Q2 frogs; leaves; stones

Q3 Boil the water to kill the germs.

Q4 1. Take the water from a river.
2. Treat the water to remove harmful germs.
3. Pipe the water to people's taps.
4. Take the used water away from houses.
5. Filter out bad things from the used water.
6. Return the filtered water to a river.

Page 6

Q1 The following reasons should be ticked: Because they deliver the water to our taps; Because they clean the water for us; Because they take our used water away.

Q2 In order, the missing words are: wells; ground; clean; flush; crops.

Q3 healthier people; more crops; better hygiene; less disease.

Section 2 — Local Traffic

Page 7

Q1

Q2 Shops — Buying things.
Banks — Using the cash machine.
Cafes — Eating and drinking.
Cinemas — Watching films.

Q3 In order, the missing words are: noisy; dirty; dangerous.

Page 8

Q1 a) counting
b) survey
c) counting
d) survey

Q2

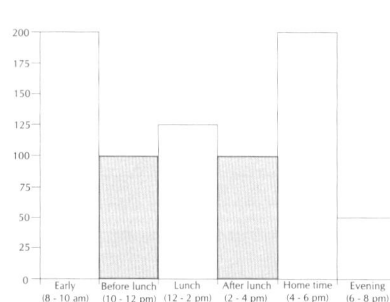

Q3 There is most traffic early in the morning and at home time — true.
In the evening lots of cars drive through the town centre — false.
The amount of traffic goes up at lunchtime compared to before and after lunch — true.

Page 9

Q1 The map and key should be shaded in as shown:

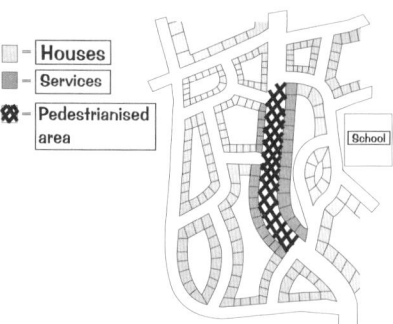

Q2 In order, the correct words and phrases are: go round the edge of; dangerous; more; noisier.

Q3 'My sales have gone down because fewer car drivers stop outside.' — Shopkeeper.
'It's much easier to buy things because you can walk from shop to shop.' — Shopper.
'We have a lot more traffic on our street now as people park here instead of in town.' — Local resident.

Page 10

Q1 The traffic through the village was very noisy. — Less traffic means life is quieter for the village residents.
Cars could only move slowly through the village. — The new bypass means traffic travels faster.
Cars caused congestion in the narrow village streets. — The new bypass can take a greater amount of traffic.

Q2 In order, the missing words are: steep; valleys; marshes; river.

Q3

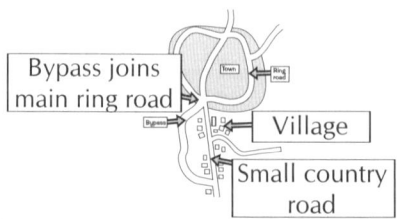

The Answers

Page 11

Q1

Q2 'The bypass has cut across my land, so I have less space for crops' — Farmer.
'I can get to my office in the town much quicker now' — Businessman.
'Our village is much quieter now the bypass has been built' — Retired Local.

Q3 Farmer — bad idea
Businessman — good idea

Page 12

Q1 The woodland is smaller and there is less room for animals — Bad.
The walk past the church is now noisy and the view has been spoilt — Bad.
Very few cars drive past the school playground now — Good.
The farmer has lost lots of good land — Bad.

Q2 In order, the missing words are: trees; noisy; tarmac; grow.

Q3 'The underpass is a smelly dark place' — sad face.
'I can never get across the bypass on my tractor' — sad face.
'Our church services are very noisy now' — sad face.

Section 3 — A Seaside Town

Page 13

Q1 Llandudno is BY THE COAST
Anglesey is AN ISLAND
Chester is in ENGLAND

Q2 a) Bangor
b) Porthmadog
c) Shrewsbury; Betws-y-coed

Q3 creates less pollution; can sit back and relax; might meet new people.

Page 14

Q1 Photo 1 — hills; town.
Photo 2 — fishing; boats.
Photo 3 — tourists; ice cream.
Photo 4 — fairground; families.

Page 15

Q1 Accommodation 9
Food & Drink 7
Leisure 4
Shopping 5
Industry 2

Q2 restaurant; cinema; bowling alley.

Page 16

Q1 In order, the correct answers are: shop; bed and breakfast; fish factory.

Q2 Mr Jones owns a boat — catches fish.
Mrs Kettle is very creative — makes craftwork.
Mrs Little is a good cook — runs a restaurant.

Q3 Mr Atkins → Mr Babbitt → Mrs Cable
Mr Douglas → Mrs Evans → Mr Freckle

Page 17

Q1 Visitors' cars cause air pollution — fresh air.
Boats can cause water pollution — clean sea water for swimming.
Visitors leave litter on the beach — beautiful beaches.
Tourism causes more buildings — lots of open space.

Q2 All Year Round — post office; newsagent; supermarket.
Tourist Season Only — fairground; craft shop; bed & breakfast.

Q3 a) teaches swimming at the local school
b) fixes machinery for the local people
c) works in the local fish factory

Page 18

Q1 In order, the following phrases complete the sentences:
there is no traffic; relaxed; on holiday; shops; at the end of; likely.

Q2 1. A lot of money comes from tourism
2. Local fishermen sell to hotels
3. Main roads lead to the beach
4. Sits between hills and the coast
5. Busier during summer

Section 4 — The Mountain Environment

Page 19

Q1 This range stretches down the west coast of North America. — Rockies.
The world's longest mountain range is in South America. — Andes.
The world's highest mountains are in the range just above India. — Himalayas.
This range in the middle of Europe is great for skiing. — Alps.

Q2 In order, the correct words are: snow; grass; valleys; farming; smaller; rounded.

Page 20

Q1 a) England
b) Irish Sea
c) Carlisle

Q2

Q3 fishing; canoeing; water-skiing; swimming; sailing

Page 21

Q1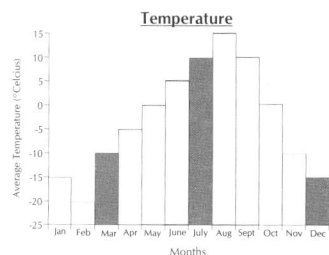

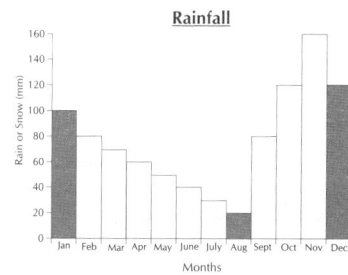

Q2 In order, the missing words are: snow; slopes; strong; snowdrifts; sliding; avalanches.

The Answers

Page 22

Q1 Snowy weather — skiing; snowboarding; tobogganing.
    Fine summery weather — rock-climbing; hiking.
Q2 In order, the following words complete the sentence: snow; summer; less busy; walking; fewer.
Q3 This is one of the most popular... — The Lake District.
    Welcome to winter paradise... — The Alps.

Page 23

Q1 local people can get jobs in resorts; local restaurants and bars have plenty of customers; local people can find jobs building resorts; local people can sell craftwork to tourists.
Q2 teaching skiing; nature guide; search and rescue; ranger.
Q3 trampling flowers; leaving litter; starting forest fires.

Page 24

Q1 Rope etc. — climbing
    Boots etc. — hiking
    Parka etc. — skiing
    Tent etc. — camping
Q2 Getting lost — Bring a map and let people know where you're going.
    Starting an avalanche — Don't ski or climb beyond warning signs.
    Suffering from injuries — Wear the correct protective clothing.
    Starving to death — Take enough food with you when hiking.
    Drowning — Take care near rivers and lakes.
Q3 a) January
    b) July
    c) October
    d) May

Section 5 — Investigating Coasts

Page 25

Q1 A. Crashing waves
    B. Headland
    C. Arch
    D. Stack
Q2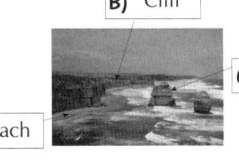

Page 26

Q1 BEACHES are shaded yellowy-brown.
    From above, STACKS are seen as lumps of rock in the sea.
    The sea is coloured BLUE.
Q2 In order, the correct places are: Rodger Trod; Sailors' Grave.

Page 27

Q1 digging a rock quarry on a cliff top
Q2 In order, the missing words are: hotel; digging; fall; cliff; crack; unstable.
Q3 a fairground; a resort hotel; a supermarket

Page 28

Q1 C → A → D → B
Q2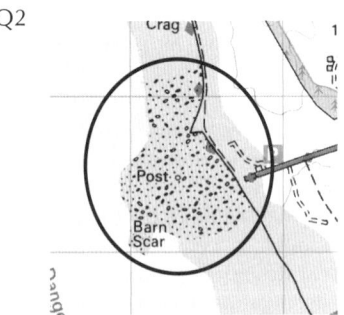

Page 29

Q1 Scary Drop Hotel — B
    Snoozy Place Hotel — A
    Soggy Nest Hotel — C
Q2 A sunbather — A beach resort
    A birdwatcher — A coastal marshland bird sanctuary
    A cliff walker — A coast with rugged cliffs

Page 30

Q1 a), c), e), f) and g) should be ticked
Q2 beach; golf course; sports centre
Q3 lions and bears — Wild Animal Attraction
    outdoor pond — Country Park
    indoor swimming pool — Leisure Centre
    science exhibit — Discovery Centre

Page 31

Q1 Houses are flooded by waves every time there's a storm. — Sea walls stop waves from splashing onto and flooding streets.
    The cliffs are weak and crumble easily. — A breakwater stops waves from crashing so hard onto cliffs.
    The sand on the beach is slowly disappearing. — Groynes (little walls) stop waves sweeping sand sideways along a beach.
Q2 a) and c) should be ticked.

Page 32

Q1 Cutting steps into the cliffs could make — the cliffs crumble into the sea.
    Using boats in the bay would create — water, air and noise pollution.
    Turning the village homes into shops would — break up the close community.
    Putting up so many new buildings would — spoil the beautiful scenery.
Q2 The following things should be ticked: more people can enjoy the seaside; more fun attractions for local people; more jobs and money for local people; more people to become friends with.

Section 6 — Passport to the World

Page 33

Q1 India — C
    Italy — A
    France — D
    UK — B
Q2 Haggis — Scotland;
    Curry — India;
    Pizza — Italy;
    Baguette — France
Q3 We've seen lions and giraffes on safari in KENYA.
    Here's me by the Leaning Tower of Pisa in ITALY.
    We're in FRANCE and I've seen the Eiffel Tower in Paris.
    I've seen kangaroos and koala bears in AUSTRALIA.

Page 34

Q1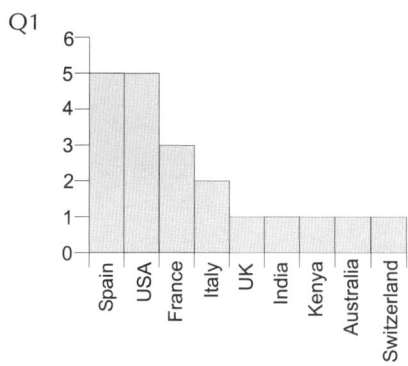

Q2 Spain and USA should be circled.
   a) 10
   b) ½
Q3 In order, the missing words and phrases are: warm sunny; beach; different from; skiing.

Page 35

Q1 In order, the correct words are: Switzerland; the USA; Norway; dry; Spain.
Q2 a)

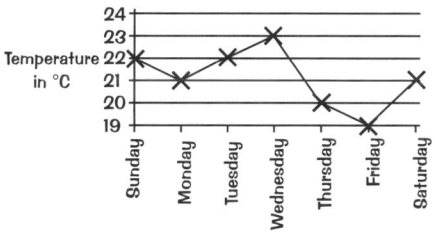

b)

Sun ☼ Mon ☼ Tues ☼ Wed Thurs Fri ☼ Sat

   c) Friday
   d) 2

Page 36

Q1 Many people die in an earthquake in India — It was a scary event and people died.
Missing local schoolgirl is found safe and well — It was a story that had a happy ending.
Australian sets new world swimming record — It was about a sporting achievement.
The president of the USA visited Glasgow today — It was about a famous person.

Q2 A Look at Mexico City — What jobs do people do here? What does the city look like?
Life with the Inuits — Where do they live? What do they eat?
The News — What's happening in the world right now?
Fab Holidays — How to get to places and what they are like.
Q3 In order, the correct words are: weather; food; poor; sunny; starvation.

Section 7 — Geography, Maps and Numbers

Page 38

Q1 a) No
   b) Yes
   c) Yes
Q2 a) A594
   b) Lorton; A66
Q3 In order, the correct words are: Knights Road; left; Maximin Road; Tollgate Road.

Page 39

Q1 In order, the correct words are: smaller; piece of paper; scale; one kilometre.
Q2 a) No
   b) Yes
   c) Yes
Q3 a) 2.5; 1.25
   b) 3

Page 40

Q1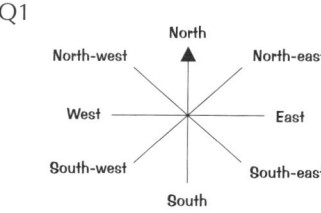

Q2 a) north-east
   b) east to west
   c) south
Q3 a) Whin Fell
   b) Dovenby
Q4 a) A school
   b) A place of worship

Page 41

Q1 Frogstop total = 5 000
   Toadham total = 50 000
Q2 Toadham is — probably a town
   Frogstop is — probably a village
   Toadham has — the most children
   Frogstop has — the fewest children
Q3

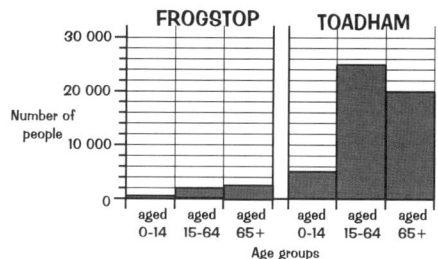

Let's face it, you want *CGP* Revision Books — not other people's dreary stuff.

Everyone else just gives you dreary revision books with only the boring stuff in and no entertainment. Boo. Hiss. We're different — we always try and make sure you're gonna enjoy using our books.

What you *really* need is a **Free Catalogue** showing the full range of CGP Revision Books. That way you can be sure you're not missing out on a brilliant book that **might just save your life**.

At CGP we **work our socks off** to despatch your stuff really quickly.
If you get your order to us before 5.00pm (Mon-Fri) you should get it next day — most of the time, anyway.
(Obviously, if you order on Saturday night on a bank holiday weekend then you won't get it 'til Wednesday morning at the very earliest — no matter how hard we try!)

FIVE ways to get your Free Catalogue really quickly

- Phone: 0870 750 1252   (Mon-Fri, 8.30am to 5.30pm)
- Fax: 0870 750 1292
- E-mail: orders@cgpbooks.co.uk
- Post: CGP, Kirkby-in-Furness, Cumbria, LA17 7WZ
- Website: www.cgpbooks.co.uk

CGP books — available in all the best bookshops

Best served with mayonnaise

ISBN 978 1 84146 751 1

G2W21

www.cgpbooks.co.uk